THIS MUST BE THE PLACE

A journey of discovery through
small-town America

Richard Sharp

Table of Contents

PROLOGUE.

On Top Of The World.

Thin mountain air has some wonderful qualities about it - in the way even the faintest of sounds take on a wistful softness and seem able to drift more easily on the breeze, becoming part of the peace rather than interrupting it; in the way the sky's blue bears a deeper hue, more pure and clear than anything I've seen before, and making me feel I can see deep into the endlessness of space; and in the way that even the slightest exertion brings about a shortness of breath which gently persuades me to take it easy, to relax and take time to soak it all in, to regard obstacles and problems as things which just come and then go, not things to be unduly flustered or troubled by, or fought or raged against. It's easier to just 'be', to be patient and go with the flow and trust that things will surely work themselves out when time is ready.

In these extraordinary places, it's always perfectly easy to see why the holy men have such a calm and confident faith in the ways of the universe.

And this calm confidence inside is very much how I'm feeling right now, as I sit perched at the top of a bank of earth and rocks on the dry and dusty roadside next to a ramshackle military checkpoint high in the Himalayan mountains; the bustling little town of Leh a few miles behind and the ultimate destination of this trip – the Khardung La pass, at an altitude of 18,380 feet, the highest motorable road in the world – just a few short miles ahead.

Short miles they may be, but at this precise moment they are also proving to be rather unattainable miles. Because this is the sort of military checkpoint where, for almost every hour of almost every day, precious little happens. As checkpoints go, there's not a great deal of checking going on. It's not really doing what it says on the tin. In fact about the only thing that's getting checked, occasionally, is the gradual passing of time.

I don't doubt that this current impasse will eventually resolve itself, so in the meantime I decide it would be prudent to invest some of the enforced downtime in checking over my bike and luggage, using the simple 'wiggle technique' to identify anything which might be on the brink of falling off. We're riding rented, and fairly ageing, Royal Enfield Bullet 500cc motorbikes, and they do have a bit of a habit of depositing various component parts along the roadside if you don't keep a close eye on things. Other bikes are, of course, available – like better built and far more reliable Japanese imports for instance; but there's a very good reason behind choosing an Enfield when riding in India, and that's the availability of backup when things go wrong. This is because across the entire subcontinent, every child over the age of five knows how to completely rebuild an Enfield from the ground up, and also has access to a large shed full of spare parts. Enfields are what keeps India moving, and consequently India is expert at keeping its Enfields moving.

Anu, our guide and mechanic and general fixer, periodically appeals to the good nature of the soldiers who consistently show not a glimmer of interest or concern, relying as so often such types do on the presence of an automatic rifle to maintain their edge of authority over the proceedings. It's funny how rifles can influence a situation. Possession of a rifle seems to completely absolve the bearer of any requirement or responsibility to engage in the conversation or take any interest in the outcome of the interaction. A simple shrug of the shoulders is all that's needed to completely halt the progress of countless people.

John, my brother-in-law and travelling companion, fiddles with the fuel pipe on his bike, kicks around some dirt, and wanders over to inspect some filthy, tar coated, archaic lump of road building machinery. John likes to inspect machinery, and there's plenty of it around to keep him occupied. It might be some of the most remote and barren and inhospitable terrain on the surface of the planet, but in this part of the world pretty much everything revolves around the road. The road is the crucial artery which connects everyone and everything. All places and people seem to need the road, and the road needs the places and the people. They are all completely interdependent. Maintaining it in something resembling serviceable condition is a constant labour; a battle to counter the forces of nature which freeze and crack it, which heat and crumble it, which deluge and wash it clean away. And so the road, and the Himalayan mountains all around us, are littered and scarred with the by-products of the endless effort which is poured into the road. With tar coated steel drums, tar coated digging and grading machines, and tar coated men whose lungs burn night and day from the caustic poison in which they toil.

The road runs for 400 miles from Manali to Leh in the Ladakh region of northern India, and then onwards over the Khardung La pass in to the Nubra Valley beyond. Massive resources are soaked up year after year to keep this ribbon of dust and rubble and tarmac intact and navigable by a never-ending procession of dilapidated Tata trucks, public buses, tourist jeeps and Indian built Enfield motorbikes. And the occasional fool on a bicycle.

And the reason for all this effort in a seemingly futile quest against the elements is of course the usual reason behind any apparent loss of reason – this road is one of only a small handful of supply routes for the troops defending the disputed territory in Kashmir against Pakistani insurgency.

This explains our current dilemma. The road over

the Khardung La is a single-track road. All roads here are single track. Normally this means that trucks and buses have no qualms about overtaking each other on blind bends above precipitous drops. But the soldiers at the checkpoint have decided that no such hazardous situation will be occurring on their watch. An army convoy is currently approaching the pass from the next valley, and so nothing must be allowed through in case we all meet in the middle with alarming, or more likely comical, consequences. Our protestations that we will have reached the summit and returned long before the crawling convoy gets anywhere near the top go unheeded. Anu's similar protests, but in slightly better Indian, also go unheeded. The uncouth Australian yeti who has joined us, apparently squeezing in the trip just in the nick of time before some cruel reversal of evolution turns him back into an ape, attempts to apply a touch of Antipodean tact and diplomacy to the situation in the form of some loud and incomprehensible ranting about the Raj and how they should be bloody grateful. He also goes unheeded. By everyone.

And then the Japanese tourists arrive.

Not, mercifully, the camera toting, golf trouser clad, middle-aged type who tend to roam in large herds; but two gushingly enthusiastic young girls in their early twenties. Judging by their private guide and their private jeep, they are roughing it in some considerable style. They are the types who have such a vast surplus of energy and excitement that they seem to bounce around the place rather than just walking in the normal fashion.

I like their refreshingly youthful and innocent attitude toward the ridiculous looking flimsy red and white painted pole, slightly bent and resting on yet another tar covered steel drum, which bars our way onward to the top of the world. You could knock it out of the way with your little finger. Obviously the guard might then see fit to shoot you, but you could definitely beat the barrier – no problem.

So they just ask the nice man to move the barrier because they want to go to the top and see the view and take some photos. The answer is 'no'. Or rather, that it is 'just not possible'. The word of some infinitely higher authority would be required for such a momentous decision as this, the making of a simple common sense concession. Blood would surely need to spilled upon the altar of the great god of bureaucracy, lest his mighty wrath be unleashed upon us and our souls condemned to damnation for all of eternity.

The girls just think it's silly, and they say so to the nice man with his shiny gun; still smiling and bouncing and clapping their hands with glee and taking photos and bouncing even more. Still the answer is no. Still they smile and bounce and plead and bounce. They keep it up for over an hour, until finally the soldiers simply can't take any more (and frankly, neither can the rest of us); and without a word one of them steps forward and the barrier is raised.

It seems that dusty bikers can be kept at bay with ease, both parties resigned to a relaxed and casual game of wait and see. A comfortable situation requiring no energy to be expended on either side, simply waiting for the solution to present itself as in time it inevitably will, it always does. But two ridiculously lively, over-enthusiastic young girls are just too much, and it's easier to let us all go and get back to the normal routine of sitting around and enjoying the peace and quiet.

We dive for our machines lest the crooked pole should fall again to thwart us. Heaving the bikes from their stands, we prime and kick the starter pedals to fire the engines into life, and rush on a wave of excitement past the guards and the barrier to resume our relentless winding climb, now fuelled with an added surge of adrenalin at the prospect that we really are going to get there. We're going to reach the top of the highest road in the world. We're going to stand at the summit and look out over what seems like the entire earth, we're going to feel the now-familiar shortness of breath and the light-headedness, and smile the smile that says 'we did it'.

At this height there's still good tarmac along most of the road surface and the riding is reasonably easy; although bikers used only to western roads should understand that, in this part of the world, good tarmac means simply that most of the road is coated in some sort of black stuff with a fairly hard crust on it. It in no way implies that any attempt has been made to smooth out whatever lies beneath it. In fact one of the most notable functions of tarmac in the Himalayas seems to be to tempt the biker up to speeds which can prove terminal for the bike and potentially the rider too when, without warning, the surface suddenly turns to loose rock or the road is cut clean through by a trench gouged out by the relentless wrecking forces of water and cold and heat.

So I ride with a moderate degree of caution, but at the same time a relaxed air as, hairpin after hairpin, the rest of the bike continues to follow more or less where the front wheel leads. By now the routine is almost completely unconscious – tapping the gear shift down into first and trailing a foot on the rear brake as I round the hairpins, each with little more of a turning radius than my examiner required me to manage two years earlier in what the bike test calls a 'u-turn'. Then twisting on the throttle out of the bend and up into second, occasionally third on a longer stretch, before slowing again and dropping the gears for the next hairpin. And so I push onwards, zigzagging continually up the last big climb, bend after bend after bend; sometimes peering down almost vertically across several loops of road to where John winds his way up behind me, sometimes picking up speed for a mile or more as the road contours around a shoulder of the mountain.

Just as familiar by now is the inevitable deterioration in the surface, as more and more rivulets and streams defy the attempts to force them down man-made culverts and instead cut straight across the road; taking tarmac, grit, stones and even small boulders over the edge and down into the valleys below. We've crossed four of these high passes already over the last few days and we know how it goes. The ruts and rocks gradually take over from the tarmac as the altitude increases, the front wheel grows ever wilder and trickier to control, and the drops get scarier too. I can feel myself becoming increasingly tense, focussing harder and harder on the bike, the road, the bends and the precipitous, disastrous end to the trip, the bike, and me which will be the inevitable result of just one small mistake.

Snow is lying all around now, sometimes banked up and reducing the road width significantly; and in places large sections have been gouged away from the edge of the road, leaving my heart in my mouth as I urge the bike through half a roads' width past another mighty, dizzying chasm dropping thousands of feet into a boulder strewn ravine. The pressure is raised still further by occasional glimpses of old machinery lying smashed and contorted among the rocks below. I wonder what became of the drivers of those old trucks whose hopeless brakes finally gave out completely, hurling them off the outside of the next bend into a thundering fall that rips apart everything but the spine of the vehicle, its prop shaft and rear axle, which mark its final resting place like a rusting steel tombstone.

An utterly barren lifelessness has spread its blanket over the land now. We left the last few scrubby trees behind us not long after the checkpoint, stooping like wizened old monks silently watching us as we rode by. Grasses and lichens and other Alpine-like plants with which I'm not familiar clung on for a few thousand feet more, but now nothing lives at all. The extreme daily routine of heating and freezing allows no noticeable plant life to exist, and leaves countless miles of cracked and split and shattered rocks like giant scree slopes which appear to form the bulk of the mountains from shortly after they leave the grassy river valleys until, many thousands of feet above, their jagged rocky peaks, streaked and speckled with snow, pierce the sky from atop these great mounds of brown rubble. It's a dramatic landscape on an infinite scale. A landscape in which it is a great privilege to travel, where it pays to treat nature with due respect, and where even non-believers like myself feel it wise to offer up the occasional prayer to smooth passage, partly because these mountains do have an intensely spiritual quality about them which makes it pretty hard to deny that something much greater than us must be operating in some way, and partly because – well you know, just in case.

I'm churning inside now. There's a huge amount of excitement and anticipation and emotion welling up in me, because at literally any moment I'm going to find that this bend is the last bend and I'm going to see the inevitable yellow painted sign which marks the top of the pass, proudly proclaiming the height of the road and the fact that the Border Roads Commission continues to hold it all just about together and make it all possible. I'm going to see that incredible view open up as the horizon suddenly seems to streak away from me, and my eyes follow it deep into the far distance in a flash as though some silent jet fighter has catapulted my whole being hundreds of miles into the view itself. But there's also another feeling which I recognise. I'm scared. Thus far the roads and the passes and the heights and drops have been exhilarating, but today things have been different. Today it's been a few clear degrees more extreme and the feeling of exposure has been very acute. As my altitude-slowed mind processes these feelings though, it seems to me that it is right and fitting that it should feel like this today. I'm happy that it has been difficult and has tested my nerve and left my heart pounding a few times too often. This is a fantastic sense of having really achieved something special. This is the highest road in the world, this is over 18,000 feet high; higher than Everest base camp, higher than the summit of any mountain peak in Europe. And we're here, on bloody motorbikes!

The next bend is the last one, and in an instant I'm right there, punching the air with my fist, screaming 'Yes', pulling up and hitting the kill switch and heaving the bike back onto its stand and swinging off and striding across to stand and stare and gasp in awe at that view. The top of the world. The top of the whole bloody world and I'm right here. John's here too, and we're grinning the widest stupidest grins you've ever seen and just soaking in so many senses and emotions that I feel quite drunk on it all.

We're also wondering why someone has seen fit to install a solitary gents urinal here. All on its own, cemented between two large boulders just a few yards off the road. As thought-provoking contemporary art installations go, it's certainly up there with the best.

The weather is fantastic, intensely bright and comfortably warm; a gentle breeze fluttering the tangled strings of prayer flags, wafting countless thousands of silent chants on the winds across the miles of deep blue sky and on into outer space, whispering to the souls of long forgotten times, who in return seem to be blessing our presence in their kingdom. There is no other way this day and this view could be here.

Today has sown a seed. I've discovered a new type of experience and I feel so fantastically exhilarated by it all. I've seen things more wonderful than I ever imagined. I didn't even try to imagine them before, as I didn't know they were there to be imagined. I simply didn't think about doing this kind of thing at all because the limit of my experiences in life just didn't go this far. We don't miss what we don't know, after all. But I've tasted what it's like now, and I know the most important thing is to keep doing it.

Embarking upon adventures like this can be quite daunting or even frightening, but what I've learned on this trip is the subtlety in the detail of that phrase. It's the *embarking* that's the most frightening part, much more so than the actual adventure itself. Of course there are a multitude of heart-stopping moments during the journey too, but when you're in you're in, and too engaged to worry about the fear all that much. I've discovered that the crossing of the threshold is the big bit, and once it's crossed everything else unfolds well enough if you trust to luck, the kindness of human nature, and bags of initiative. And, not surprisingly, the more you experience, the more initiative it generates within you.

I know with absolute certainty that now I must start to think about the next adventure, to look forward and to make plans. Where should it be? Which part of the world comes next?

Myself (left) and John at the Khardung
La pass, Ladakh, India.

18th April.

New Surroundings.

I t's dusk as the wheels of the 747 screech onto the runway, and fully dark by the time I've made my way through the tedious endurance test that is US customs and immigration and I'm walking hesitantly out of the arrivals hall and into the jostling lanes of buses and limos and pickup trucks and taxis and noise and urgency of LAX - Los Angeles International Airport. I'm not sure where to go or where to queue or who to ask. But that newfound faith in things turning out fine, that sense of self-assuredness, is here with me and inside I feel calm and confident. This is going to be the world as experienced on my terms, and it feels good. Right now I don't know my bearings, but I have no doubt that very soon I will, and during the period in between - who knows what interesting and unexpected things may happen.

This is the mantra I've been repeating to myself, over and over, all the time I've been planning and organising this trip. To be honest, it's amounted to quite a lot of organising and very little planning; but more of that later. The mindset of being confident, having faith, keeping calm and all that other stuff is, thus far, all theoretical. It's how I know I want to be, how I need to be, but not yet how I naturally am. I've had a taste of it, a kind of trial run, and it felt good so I want to adopt it full time and live by it. But it's hardly tested or proven, and by no means the norm yet. I've got to stick with it though, or the next few weeks are likely to go horribly wrong in so many ways.

A few minutes later I've got the measure of the place and I'm sliding into the worn and rather tattered leather rear seat of a yellow taxi and saying 'Santa Monica Boulevard please' through the slightly worrying steel wire grille which separates the driver from the crazed lunatics in the back. Without thinking, I drop the 't' in 'Santa' and it comes out in a dreadful version of an American drawl, which is utterly pointless anyway as my driver is Azerbaijani and speaks very little English, very badly. As we thread our way through the intimidating and ugly road system which seems to be a universal design template of the immediate hinterland of every international airport, I take in my first sights and sounds of real America. The cars and buildings and relentless advertising create an instant impact, and it's exciting to be here. Neon is everywhere, and thundering great gas guzzling cars, and I can't really quite believe this is me sitting right here in the thick of it, getting my first proper taste of the adventure I've spent almost a year researching and looking forward to. There haven't actually been any maps plastered to my walls and peppered with post-it notes and coloured pins joined up by lengths of string, but a great number of books have been read and mental notes made of places to keep an eye out for, and so now I have an extensive knowledge of the history and folklore connected with the route I'm about to travel. In terms of practical arrangements, I've booked a hotel room for tonight, a flight home in about six weeks' time, and of course I've arranged to rent a bike. That's the full extent of the forward planning.

Having learned the Azerbaijani phrases and hand signals for 'excuse me sir, I believe you may not have noticed I wish to pull out' and 'I'd prefer it if you didn't stop in front of me like that', I'm eventually delivered in relative safety to the front door of the entirely insalubrious Comfort Inn on Santa Monica Boulevard. Inside the tired looking reception area, and after one of those awkward waits where you start to wonder whether the button you pressed is actually connected to a bell anywhere, but you're afraid to press it again for fear of causing offense, I'm greeted by a very friendly and courteous young Spaniard who smiles and immediately boosts my confidence in the plan by confirming that I do indeed have a reservation and showing me to my clean(ish), simple yet functional bedroom. It's neither comfortable nor homely, but it's adequate and of a standard that I've a feeling I'm soon going to get quite used to. I throw the bags onto the bed and just stand for a moment looking out of the grubby window into the floodlit car park and running a quick thought process through my head - firstly just to confirm to myself that I'm really here, in a motel room in Santa Monica, about to set out on the sort of adventure that most people never get the chance to experience, or never muster the initiative to try; and second, to clarify in my rather travel-wearied mind that what I ought to do next and what I *am* going to do next are two entirely different things. I should unpack my things, check through the paperwork for the bike hire, and generally take stock and get myself properly organised. So I'm going to have a quick shower and head straight out for a couple of beers.

Thirty minutes later I'm strolling down the broad concrete pavement, thinking that I really ought to refer to it as a sidewalk from now on, passing palm trees every few yards and drawing the fresh sea air into my nostrils, and noticing how the grass is different here – it's that course and rather sparsely growing stuff you always get in hotter climates, with pop up sprinklers dotted here and there. The mere name of the road, Santa Monica Boulevard, sounds amazing to me. Santa Monica Boulevard, I say it again under my breath, isn't it just wonderful? It evokes thoughts of Eric Clapton's brilliant 461 Ocean Boulevard and takes me back to being a teenager in the mid 1970's, when I remember gazing at the sleeve of that album and imagining what a wonderfully exotic place it must be. In actual fact, the particular Ocean Boulevard in question is where Clapton was living at the time he recorded the album, in the town of Golden Beach,

Florida, which of course is on completely the opposite side of America. But let's not allow minor geographical details to get in the way of romantic notions. I'm walking through a scene which completely and perfectly epitomises exactly what I imagined this part of America to be – the warm sea breeze, the infinitely wide and palm lined boulevard, the occasional huge pickup trucks with booming and burbling exhaust notes from monstrous engines which must consume the entire fuel output of a small middle eastern nation in just the distance from one traffic light to the next.

But much as Santa Monica Boulevard makes its unforgettable impression on me as my first real footfall on this great adventure, this road actually has another name; a name which is famous the world over, and which encapsulates a spirit of adventure and freedom and wanderlust. This road is Route 66. This really is it. This broad strip of concrete I'm walking along right now is the last half mile or so of the road which has been the sole focus of my attention and energy and excitement for most of the previous twelve months. This, right here where I'm standing, is about the point where, throughout the 50's and 60's and 70's, countless thousands of bright and beautiful young things caught their first glimpse of the sea and the funfairs and beaches which they sought as they drove their Mustangs and T-Birds many hundreds, often thousands, of miles to reach the sun and the surf, almost certainly listening to the Beach Boys on their eight track cassette players every inch of the way. And earlier in the century, during the great depression of the 1930's, here was journey's end for so many desperate and hungry refugees from the great dustbowl, leaving the ravaged and wasted farmlands of Oklahoma in their battered jalopies, bringing everyone and everything they had to California, the promised land, which for so many of them just couldn't deliver - for those of you who have read John Steinbeck's 'The Grapes Of Wrath' will know that Route 66 wasn't just the glittering route to the sun for the generation of 60's America who first learned how to have serious fun. The Mother Road had its first incarnation and rise to fame, or rather notoriety, in an altogether tougher age, when it was anything but the romantic image most associate with it today and instead became the road of broken dreams, the artery which spilled the lifeblood out of the dustbowl states, the unimaginably harsh journey to a false Shangri-La which was already overcrowded and would end in even more desperation, pain and exploitation than that which the travellers had left behind.

Route 66 is, without doubt, the most famous road in the world, and here I am walking right along it. How cool is that?

I don't really know how much further it is to the seafront, so I resolve to save that pleasure until the morning and instead walk straight into the first bar which presents itself, which is a slightly seedy but just about acceptable looking establishment by the name of McCabe's, the frontage of which simply states 'Bar,

Eats, Pool'. This sounds exactly what I'm in need of, and stepping inside it's just perfect – with those pointless swinging saloon doors and a few kids playing pool on tables with outrageously garish coloured baize, and an enormous square bar surrounded by fixed revolving stools forming the central focus of the room.

'Hoo ya doon pal' enquires the landlord, in not quite the accent I was expecting.

'Very well thanks, and I don't think you're American are you?'

'Aye yer reet there son, Glasgie, and aam thinkin yoos'll be a Sassenach but al noo hold that agin ye'.

Colin McCabe is a tough looking ex-pat Glaswegian whose nose has evidently collided with quite a few fists in its time, and who has clearly learned how to create the fully authentic 'dive bar' experience. He's also learned how to serve beer the American way, as freezing cold Bud is poured into a freezing cold glass, and the first one barely touches the sides on the way down.

So here I am, sitting five thousand miles from home, drinking beer served by a Scottish landlord, and flanked at the bar by two east London lads sporting ghastly nylon English football club shirts while watching the Arsenal vs Blackburn game on satellite television. Welcome to America!

Although I'm surrounded by people and inside I'm buzzing with excitement, I also have a feeling of slight detachment from my immediate surroundings, as though either I or they are not quite real. I strike up an intermittent conversation with Colin (the football supporters are incapable or uninterested, or possibly both) which drifts from motorbikes to Scotland to expat living and around again several times, and all the while I'm not really at all engaged in the conversation, not there in the moment, and he probably thinks me a little simple or more likely rude. Thinking about it, it's probably just down to the length of time I've been awake. I'm not really capable of making the effort necessary to keep the conversation flowing, so I let it slide and am more than content to quietly sip a couple more beers and just soak in my surroundings and the feeling of being on the brink of something extraordinary.

After finally conceding the futile battle with jet lag and retiring to bed at last, I lie gazing at the ceiling for a while, reflecting on what a long day of cramped travelling it's been. In fact it would have been more than a day if the time hadn't been wound back by eight hours while I was in the air. I marvel at how it's possible to experience such a dramatic change in culture and surroundings in just the space of a day, from a rural railway station in northern England to the bright lights of Los Angeles, just a stone's throw from the Pacific Ocean.

I smile as the thought occurs to me that although I've now been in the country for several hours, I haven't actually managed to find a real American person yet.

It isn't long before the deep sleep of exhaustion claims me.

19th April. 100 miles.

Getting Acquainted.

I'm awake and showered early, almost shaking with a heady mix of excitement and barely controlled terror, and by 7 o'clock I'm already delicately attempting to coax something resembling a cup of coffee from the flimsy equipment supplied on my hospitality tray. Having failed to operate the stupid machine correctly I've spilled hot water all over the tray, the coffee and sugar sachets, the floor and a towel; and am now stirring the remnants with a useless plastic stick which is rapidly melting into a floppy and twisted mess. It's becoming abundantly clear that I need to get out into the real world beyond these drab motel walls and place breakfast firmly in the hands of professionals!

Today is the day I shall collect the bike, my travelling companion for the next six weeks and goodness knows how many thousand miles. But the rental depot doesn't open till 10.00 so I have plenty of time on my hands before I need to head across town.

Outside, the early morning air smells wonderful. Everywhere is fresh and watered and ready for the first warmth of the sun, and that includes me. It turns out to be about a quarter of a mile walk to the end of the road, the sea front of Santa Monica, and what has been journey's end for so many. Exhausted refugees hunting the promised land and fun seekers ready to start the holiday party, they all spilled out of these last few yards of Route 66 and onto the stunning expanse of pale golden sand just as I'm doing this morning – except for me this isn't the end. Far from it, because being a bit of a contrary sort I've decided to travel in the opposite direction to most other people, and so their end of the road is to be my beginning. There are actually two very good reasons why I've decided to travel from west to east; the first being that it means the late afternoon sun will be behind me rather than right in my eyes as I ride, and the second being that as it's only April it makes sense to stay further south where it's warmer to begin with and then travel gradually north as the weeks go by. A great theory I reckon, and one which is destined to unravel in emphatic style over the next few weeks!

Just as the guidebooks promised, here is the plaque dedicated to Will Rogers:

Will Rogers Highway / Dedicated 1952 to Will Rogers / Humorist – World Traveler – Good Neighbor / This Main Street Of America / Highway 66 / Was The First Road He Traveled In A Career The Led Him Straight To The Hearts Of His Countrymen.

They can't spell, that's for sure. And what with 'The Mother Road', the 'Will Rogers Highway', and the 'Main Street of America', they have an awful lot of alternative names for a road which surely needs only one name – Route 66.

I stroll out onto the beach, a painstakingly manicured version of what is naturally a beautiful expanse of sand. I've had a rather romantic notion in my head that I will pick up a pebble from this beach and keep it in my pocket all the way across America, and ultimately toss it back into the sea when I reach the furthest point of my journey, somewhere on the eastern seaboard. I didn't plan, however, for the Southern Californian obsession with tidiness, where randomly placed footprints in the sand simply cannot be tolerated, where excited children's sandcastles cannot be allowed to stand too long, lest their chaotic architecture should undermine the proper sense of adult neatness and order. So here, at around 8.00 every morning, watched by the hazy eyes of the winos and the beggars, the beach manicuring brigade are hard at work with their tractors towing giant rakes and rollers, smoothing and polishing every individual grain of sand so as to appear at its very best, at just the right angle and in just the right light. We are, it should be remembered, very close to Hollywood.

It's soon clear that with this obsession for immaculate presentation, no grubby little pebble is going to be allowed to disrupt the polished veneer or risk causing discomfort to the tender foot of California. A pebble in this pristine sand would, I suspect, be about as acceptable as a deeply furrowed wrinkle on an otherwise perfectly Botox-ed forehead. So it takes me the best part of an hour, and an excursion which ends in me rooting around like some tramp beneath the rusting and barnacle encrusted piles of the pier, before I succeed in locating my elusive pebble. And it's not exactly the polished gem of a stone I had hoped for either. Oh America, what have you done with your priorities that it takes me so long to find a tiny imperfection in your natural environment, yet all the time I'm watched with curious intrigue by the abandoned, the hopeless, and the pissed?

With my first mission successfully accomplished and the pebble finally in my pocket, I stroll along the wooden boards of the famous Santa Monica Pier, symbol of arrival for generations of travellers and revellers; be they the rich, the poor or the destitute. We had piers like this once in England, but after their Victorian heyday had passed we forgot to look after them anymore and they gradually vanished one by one, lost either to corrosion, suspicious fires, or both. The British coastline once boasted over a hundred of these beautiful structures, but sadly today less than half of them remain standing, most of them in an increasingly perilous state of disrepair. Santa Monica, by contrast and to its great credit, has taken good care of its pier, and I'm glad. It's got candy floss stalls and a funfair complete with a roller coaster and ferris wheel, and a fine looking seafood restaurant at the end; and it's exactly what a proper pier should be. Were it in England, its primary attractions would be a ramshackle shed selling Kiss-Me-Quick hats, along with an oddly decorated doorway advertising the services of a fortune telling gypsy. And probably a few areas of serious rot and a 'keep out' sign too.

It's still early, and this is a town where nothing, and I mean absolutely nothing, happens before 10.00 am. So after a little hunting around it seems that the only available option for breakfast is the Georgian Hotel, a masterpiece of art deco design and both original and perfect in every detail. A table on the elegant elevated veranda, looking across the beachside boulevard to palm trees, golden sands, and the Pacific Ocean, combined with poached eggs topped with lobster sauce, and a cappuccino which is vastly superior to the frothy rubbish we're served in England, and I'm rapidly starting to enjoy my day.

The climbing sun begins to deliver its spring warmth, the beach slowly comes alive with the beautiful citizens of Los Angeles, those who have sweated for their looks and those who have just paid the surgeon, and my mind is awash with thoughts of what a wonderful life this is, how lucky I am, and how excited I feel about what lies ahead. Apprehensive too, but a strong sense of calmness is also present, the fledgling stages of my growing belief that when you just get on and throw yourself into a situation, things will undoubtedly work out, and the 'right way' will always somehow reveal itself.

Another cappuccino, because I sort of know that the quality of the coffee will more than likely go downhill from here, and it's time to get active. Back to the motel, bags collected and a taxi ride across town to find the Eaglerider Harley-Davidson Rental Company on the rather enchanting sounding La Cienega Boulevard. But this particular dose of enchantment turns out to be a sprawling and not especially prosperous looking commercial district, squeezed in amongst a network of concrete freeway flyovers about a mile or so from the airport.

I'm welcomed by a really friendly bunch of people though, including Claudio with whom I've been exchanging emails for some months – I send emails, he doesn't respond, I call:

'Hi Claudio, it's Richard, from England'

'Hey, good day to you sir, and how can I help you today?'

'I was just ringing to check you got my emails about the panniers and luggage rack on the bike.'

'You want to rent a bike?'

'Yes we've already arranged that. I've booked a bike and paid you for it. Mr Sharp? Six weeks? One way to Boston, Massachusetts?'

'Oh yeah, sure, I got you now. How you doin' sir?'

'I'm very well thanks. Just wondering if you got my emails about the panniers?'

'Yeah sure we did, everything's all good to go sir.'

'Ok thanks, so no problems with the panniers?'

'You want panniers? Yeah that'll be no problem sir. Could you just confirm that request by email?'

'Yes, like I said, I've already emailed you about panniers, but I didn't hear back from you so I wondered whether you'd got the message'.

At this point I'd concluded it would save a lot of time and further transatlantic telephone bills to just wait till I got here.

Meeting Claudio in the flesh for the first time, I now understand his apparent lack of attention to detail. He's a good looking young lad in his mid-twenties at a guess, olive skinned and with his shirt unbuttoned far enough to reveal a smoothly shaved and lightly oiled chest, clearly of Italian origin, and clearly far more focussed on his appearance and irresistibility to the ladies than he is on the job in hand. He can certainly turn on the charm though, and that gets around any amount of administrative neglect.

The mechanics have obviously taken plenty of trouble to clean and service the bike for me though, and it's sitting there proud and pretty as hell in the middle of the car park. I've chosen to ride a Harley-Davidson Dyna Wide Glide, not because it's the best suited to touring large distances, far from it, in fact they thought I was raving mad wanting this model; no, I chose it for just one simple reason – because it's the most gorgeous and coolest looking lump of metal I've ever had the pleasure of setting eyes upon.

Up until just a few months ago I was working as a sales rep for a company which organised conferences. I'd had an enquiry from Harley-Davidson's UK head-quarters about helping to stage their European dealer conference, to be held in a swanky hotel on the shores of Lake Maggiore in Italy, and I was on my way to visit their offices near London and pitch my ideas. Fortuitously, the day before the meeting I happened to find myself parked outside the Harley dealership on the Kings Road in Chelsea, and not knowing the first thing about motorbikes I decided it would be ten minutes well spent to pop in and have a nose around. Plus I might even wangle a free coffee.

I walked through the door and was confronted by the most beautiful work of art I've ever seen, right there in front of me. Gleaming chrome, wild glittering paintwork, deliciously elegant yet functional lines, simply oozing quality and engineering excellence; all working in harmony to create the epitome of a true thoroughbred.

I'd never ridden a bike before, never even been on the back of one. But what I saw then, in just the brief-est of moments, made up my mind about something – I had to have one. Within twelve months I'd learned to ride, passed my test, and bought myself that very bike. And I was 39 at the time. To me, this thing is complete perfection. It's solid and practical engineering in a form so pure and simple that it's become an iconic design classic. Nature may have created the leopard, but Harley-Davidson have created the Dyna Wide Glide. Both perfect at what they do, both beautiful beyond words.

It has to be said though, that the Harley-Davidson brand is one that sharply divides opinion - people either love them or hate them, and there's no middle ground. But for those who love them, you'll struggle to find a brand with a more loyal and devoted following. Did you know that the Harley-Davidson 'bar and shield' logo is tattoed onto the skin of its devotees in greater numbers than any other brand in the world? As brands go, it's certainly been around a while too. The 'bar and shield' logo was first introduced in 1910, just seven years after William Harley and Arthur Davidson built their first production motorcycle in a ten foot by fifteen foot shed in Milwaukee, and it remains virtually unchanged to the present day.

Back to the here and now though, and much as the bike sitting in front of me looks great, the pannier bags, which I'm amazed to see they have actually fitted to it (someone evidently did get the message, even if Claudio doesn't recall passing it on) are absolutely crap. Old, sagging and far too small, and with great long bolts sticking out ready to snag and rip anything I might try to stuff into them.

After a little discussion, Claudio determines that it will be easier to change the bike than change the bags, so an alternative machine is wheeled from the garage – identical in every detail except for a line of dents along the lower of the twin exhaust pipes, presumably the result of a rather embarrassing mishap by some previous rental customer. Well, it has character, and it has decent panniers, so it's now my trusty steed for the next six weeks.

I load up and strap on my bags, badly, and away we head into the traffic of the Los Angeles freeways with recent news reports of unprovoked highway shootings still echoing in my head, a head scantily protected for the moment by a very dodgy helmet which they supplied with the bike, and which lacks a few of the basic features one might reasonably expect like a visor and a serviceable buckle. By the time I'm travelling at 40 miles per hour, even sheltered by sunglasses, my eyes are already streaming so badly that I can't see properly, and this isn't great given that I've launched myself straight into the lunchtime traffic on the approaches to the airport. Luckily, I am of course in a large and wealthy city in America, which means that a Harley-Davidson dealership will be only a matter of a few minutes along the road. Sure enough, I'm soon signing the credit card slip and a shiny new helmet is mine, complete with flip down visor, a buckle which actually works, and a ridiculous great big number '1' on the back, gaudily decorated with the stars and stripes. Ah well, it fits fine and the visor is great, and when it's on my head I can't see what an idiot I look. Let's face it, for America, it's actually a fairly conservative design and not one person ever comments on it during the whole of my trip as it turns out.

I deliberate whether I should waste half an hour dropping the original helmet back with Claudio or do his future customers a favour by consigning it to the nearest bin. Rubbish though it is, it was also the best one on the shelf, so I decide I'd better return it.

Back out onto the freeway – I must remember to call them freeways now rather than motorways, freeways and sidewalks, welcome to the US of A – and I'm soon relishing the ability to see where I'm going and feeling quite comfortable and relaxed on the road. I pass the pier and the Georgian Hotel and carry on along the coast road, quickly leaving the city behind and getting a true taste of the American idyll as I cruise through the jet set retreat of Malibu, with the Pacific surf rolling in wave after perfect wave onto the immaculate golden sands. I'm planning to spend the rest of the day just having an easy run up and back down the coast, getting the feel of the bike and the roads, tweaking the luggage, and making sure everything about it seems in perfect working order before I turn east and leave the Pacific behind me once and for all. My rental includes breakdown cover, but I'd still rather be sure that everything's just so before I head off into the unknown.

It's wonderful riding, with a warm breeze in my face, feet up on the foot pegs in front, suitably stylish and understated leather jacket, and the obligatory

Raybans of course. This is California's famous Highway 1, the Pacific Coast Highway, one of the world's most beautiful coastal roads, snaking its way up the stunning coastline to San Francisco and beyond. The roadside verges are all sandy, with tall spindly palm trees swaying gently and lots of spiky cactus-like plants in amongst scrubby vegetation; it all feels incredibly exotic and exhilarating. Today I only ride as far as the big naval base at Port Hueneme before turning back south, but not before making a mental note that there's the makings of another epic trip to be done here.

I make a few more stops for photos and luggage tweaking before finding myself back on the Santa Monica seafront, where I pull into a suitably cheap looking motel and park up next to a group of half a dozen seriously smart Harleys. Each one looks as though its owner must have browsed through the accessories catalogue for many a long hour before eventually thinking 'what the heck, I'll just take the lot'. I reckon with all these glistening beasts to choose from, no decent bike thief is going to give mine a second glance.

The motel owner relieves me of $65 in return for some dodgy wiring and a carpet bearing the most extraordinary number of cigarette burns, so I don't linger in the room and am soon tucked into a cosy booth in a Mexican restaurant half way along the pier.

I ask the waitress for a cold beer, and order enchiladas with refried beans on her recommendation.

'And would you like Super Salad to begin?' she enquires.

'Just the main I think, thank you.'

I reflect on my first day's adventures while enjoying the excellent meal. I'm very happy with the bike and how all the gear has fitted onto it, and already I feel remarkably relaxed and comfortable on the American roads. They really do seem to be a nation of calm and considerate drivers, a far cry from what you'll be told by anyone around the world who doesn't know what they're talking about, and without exception they admire the wonderful lines and sparkling chrome of the bike. I feel quite confident now about navigating my way through the heart of Los Angeles tomorrow. It takes the pressure off, knowing it's always easy to pull over just about anywhere when a little consultation of the map is called for.

Everything about the bike seems to be absolutely spot on. It runs beautifully, all the levers are adjusted just right for me (you sometimes need to alter things like the angle of the gear shift or the rear brake pedal), and despite extensive prodding and wiggling I can't find anything which looks like it might come loose. I've also got to grips with how best to stow all the gear, although I'll try the holdall across the back seat rather than the luggage rack tomorrow, just to spread the load a bit more evenly, and then keep my small rucksack on my back with things like passport and paperwork and guidebooks – all the stuff I either need frequently or simply can't risk losing. I do need to keep it fairly light though, as for some reason my left shoulder is aching rather badly and I only rode 100 miles today, which is a little worrying.

Malibu was perhaps the only minor disappointment today. Whereas I'd expected the capital of cool, instead there was no real sense of 'place' at all. Just a long coastal road lined with the big heavy ornate gates of multi-million dollar mansions which presumably hid the rich and famous and beautiful, interspersed with a handful of open areas fronting various beaches and lined with the camper vans of the not quite so rich.

Belly full, I meander slowly back to the motel, taking in the warm salty smell of the sea and noting that along Ocean Avenue, as the seafront road is imaginatively named, the palm trees and the tramps come in more or less equal numbers.

I need to sleep long and deeply, but of course I don't.

20th April. 150 miles.

On The Road.

The first day on Route 66! I'm awake at 6.30 and wishing I'd slept better. My aching shoulder prevented me sleeping properly, although I'm sure excitement and anticipation had just as much to do with it as well. Anyway, I've no time or inclination to moan about sore body parts, because this is the big adventure and it starts right now.

As soon as I'm up and dressed, my first job is to check the tyres. It's occurred to me that, with all the messing about over the rubbish panniers and ending up swapping the bike at the last minute, I'd completely forgotten to have a good look at the condition of the rubber on the replacement machine I'm now riding. You see, whilst you might reasonably expect to get up to 15,000 miles out of a typical car tyre, you're doing well to get much more than a third of that from a bike tyre, which means I'm going to be pushing this limit pretty hard by the end of my journey if I'm to avoid wasting the best part of a day getting them changed. The reason for this huge difference in durability, by the way, is simply that the rubber compound used in bike tyres needs to be a lot stickier, and therefore softer, than car tyres to compensate for the much smaller footprint which is in contact with the tarmac and still provide a decent amount of grip.

I'm pleased to find the tyres are so new that the little rubber hairs from the moulding process are almost all still present; so I return to my room, somewhat relieved not to have hit an obstacle before I've even started, to get packed and ready to go.

Loading up the bike, I chat for a while with the affluent looking owners of the fancy bikes I'm parked next to. They're a bunch of old friends who've congregated from various corners of the state, and they're on their way to a big bike rally in Laughlin, all decked out in their tough looking biker leathers with studs and tassels, and sporting bandanas and aviator shades, none of which show the slightest sign of having accumulated any road grime or other form of wear and tear. It doesn't really strike me as being their normal attire; they look slightly uncomfortable and self-conscious, rather like they're wearing a fancy dress outfit that only comes out of the cupboard on special occasions, and they're not completely convinced that they look the epitome of cool rather than just silly. But who am I to pass judgement, decked out in my stars and stripes helmet? I conclude quite quickly that they're probably all solicitors and accountants and the like, whose wives allow them to go off and play Easy Rider for one weekend every year, and whose bikes will probably clock up less mileage in their lifetimes than mine will on this single trip. I pretend I know where Laughlin is and all about the rally, because it's clear that any proper biker should know this, and wish them all well with their middle class hell raising. They guess from my accent that I'm Australian and, when duly corrected, proceed to congratulate me at length for having elected such an intelligent prime minister (historical note – it was Tony Blair at the time, and as they had George Bush in power it wasn't too hard to appear intelligent).

I can't resist one last coffee at the Georgian as it's only a few yards up the road, and then at 9.00 o'clock I thumb the start switch and the big V-twin pumps its booming throb through the dented exhausts to reverberate around the enclosed courtyard. I squeeze in the heavy clutch lever, dab my left toe on the gear shift, feel the clunk and judder as first is engaged, and in a few moments I'm rolling up Santa Monica Boulevard, Route 66, my almost constant companion for the next few weeks.

My surroundings become steadily more affluent and glitzy as I travel towards and through Beverly Hills, with designer boutiques, expensive restaurants, and prestige car showrooms lining the road; and then deteriorate rapidly and slightly unnervingly beyond the district of West Hollywood. When I eventually glimpse the famous HOLLYWOOD sign on the hillside away to my left, it's from the kind of road junction where I really don't want the lights to stay on red for too long, as a group of very shifty characters eye me up and down thoughtfully, calculating the odds. This is definitely too early in the journey to become a crime statistic.

My route for the first part of the day, cautiously picking my way and negotiating the heart of Los Angeles, is carefully studied and committed to memory. I'm trying to follow as close as possible to the course of the old road, which isn't always very easy in areas where decades of urban development have steadily reshaped the road layout. I follow Route 66, aka Santa Monica Boulevard, also aka Highway 2 just around here, until it meets Highway 101 which I take for a couple of miles into central LA, marvelling at all the signs for places like Paramount Studios, the Dodger Stadium, and MacArthur Park. Then it's back onto proper Route 66 again in its modern-day guise as Highway 110 out to Pasadena, another very affluent area where a brief stop to check the map doesn't carry with it quite the same risk of a mugging or drive-by shooting.

Here I try out my first American petrol pump, and not without some considerable difficulty. They just don't work the same as ours do, what with slots for your credit card, requests for your zip code which of course isn't recognised, and an initially rather baffling sort of sliding mechanism on the nozzle which has to be held back to allow the fuel to flow.

A very brief spell on Interstate 210 and I pick up the

original course of old Route 66 again in the form of Colorado Boulevard, and then the aptly named Foothill Boulevard, which I'm pleased to find is at last actually designated with the number 66, for about forty miles of dead straight road running along the beautiful base of the San Gabriel mountains, with their tree covered slopes in the foreground backed by snow-capped peaks which shimmer incongruously through a Southern Californian heat haze.

Foothill Boulevard might also be called Traffic Light Boulevard. There are hundreds of the bloody things, and my left hand and forearm quickly become so tired from working the heavy clutch lever that I'm grimacing with determination at every gear change, and eventually crunching through the gears without the help of the clutch whenever I can get away with it (it's not too hard to do this on a bike – you just have to synchronise flicking the gear shifter with a quick blip of the throttle). Why the hell can't Harley make a nice light clutch mechanism just like everyone else can though?

On another practical note, the budding traveller should be aware that although the guidebooks promise lots of nice clear 'Route 66' signs along the roads through Los Angeles, there are in fact none at all. I'm already well beyond Pasadena before I happen across my first one, and I'm so surprised to see it that I almost run over a startled pensioner.

The Los Angeles urban sprawl continues through

Arcadia, La Verne, Claremont, and the wonderfully named Rancho Cucamonga, where I join Interstate 15 in order to cut out a few miles of traffic lights and bypass San Bernadino (home of the world's very first McDonald's restaurant if you're interested - so probably well worth a miss) and head up into the mountains towards the Cajon Pass.

The change in surroundings is sudden and dramatic. Abruptly, the buildings are all gone, and there's an eight lane highway carving up a beautiful river valley, flanked by high peaks and strange rock formations. I stop for some lunch at the Summit Inn, a fantastic old 1950's American diner at the top of the Cajon Pass, where I'm somewhat taken aback to discover that I've climbed from sea level to over 4,000 feet this morning. The diner is an absolute gem, little changed since its heyday I imagine, and still with the wonderful old fixed bar stools along the counter and a waitress who chews gum and wears one of those rather quaint little paper hats in a red and white gingham check pattern. Around the walls hang what is soon to become a very familiar sight of assorted Route 66 memorabilia, bits of old Chevy's, weathered signposts, and general junk. I battle my way valiantly through almost half of a vast club sandwich and chips (sorry, fries) before wandering outside to admire some lovely rusty old fuel trucks and click off a few arty photos. If the Summit Inn is a taste of what's to come, I'm going to love it.

I'm back onto Interstate 15 for only a couple more

miles before branching off to Victorville where old Route 66 reappears in grand style, well signposted this time and looking just the way it should – worn and cracked, dusty, largely forgotten, but very much still hanging in there.

From Victorville, the old road loops away from the Interstate and also parts company with the twenty first century. First passing through the run down mining town of Oro Grande, and then the almost non-existent Helendale, and twenty or so miles later into Barstow, this stretch provides the first classic scenes of the ageing tarmac stretching away ahead of me for as far as the eye can see. The land here is flat and featureless with nothing for the road to curve around; so it doesn't, it remains perfectly straight for miles at a time. Images exactly like this are what's got me so excited about the trip; and seeing the real thing for the first time, actually riding through it, is just an amazing experience. It really is truly wonderful, and worthy of a good few more scenic photo stops.

A little way beyond Oro Grande I come across the first of the countless quirky sights along Route 66, this one in the form of Elmer Long's Bottle Tree Ranch, a bizarre kind of sculpture park covering a couple of acres of scrub and almost entirely created from empty wine and beer bottles along with assorted bits of farm machinery and advertising signs. Elmer has, for reasons best known to himself, devoted many years to constructing innumerable steel structures adorned with bottles, many of which bear a passing resemblance to trees or even giant cacti, and topped off with oddments ranging from rifles to bedsteads and aeroplane propellers.

Beyond Helendale I gain a travelling companion for a while in the form of a freight train emblazoned with Santa Fe Railroad livery, rumbling along the tracks a few yards to my left. I engage in a little cerebral exercise to try and work out how long it is; first pacing the train to establish its speed, then accelerating to get far enough ahead that I can pull over and time how long it takes to pass a conveniently placed signal. I calculate the train to be over one and a half miles long. They really don't do half measures over here.

It's late afternoon and I've got very tired arms and shoulders as I arrive in Barstow, which consists of one big long street lined with motels and the odd restaurant, all in various stages of terminal decline. I've done 150 miles of Route 66, which doesn't come anywhere near qualifying as a big day, but the endless clutch squeezing and stopping and starting thanks to all those traffic lights this morning has taken its toll and I'm happy to call it a day.

Following a hot tip from my guidebook I search out the El Rancho Motel, described as a particularly authentic Route 66 landmark which has been 'recently restored'. On this basis, I'd place the guidebook at around 20 years out of date, as the place is a flea pit on the verge of collapse.

A ten minute exploratory trundle up and down the

main street, eyeing up the general state of repair of each motel I pass and assessing which is the least likely to be infested with cockroaches, leads me to select the Stardust Inn. Its design inspiration appears to have been the kind of stacked up arrangement of Portakabins which you often find acting as the offices on construction sites, but it's clean and comfy and at $30 it's less than half the price of last night, and there's barely a single cigarette burn in sight. All along the hotel's boundary wall is carefully painted the legend 'The friendship of those we serve is the foundation of our progress'. Hmmm, very deep.

Barstow is first and foremost (ok, solely) what they call a railroad town, or 'major transportation hub' if you want to dress it up a little like the town's mayor clearly does, so from my room I enjoy a panoramic view not only of the beginning of the Mojave Desert, but also vast acres of railway tracks and sidings. I hope there's a good sleep coming up, as tomorrow I have grand plans to detour away from Route 66 and try to get all the way through Death Valley and on to Las Vegas. I need to be successful too, as in terms of the complete lack of potential stop-over points, it looks like being one of those routes which, once you've started, you've got to finish.

I fancy a quick dinner and an early night, and the first vaguely acceptable looking restaurant along the main street turns out to be Mexican, again. Not to worry, it's good wholesome stuff.

'Help yourself to Super Salad from the buffet bar over there, and your main will be along shortly' smiles the very cheerful waitress.

I'm a little intrigued by this Super Salad thing now, although I opt to just sip a beer and wait for the main course, confidently anticipating that its size will lead me to regret having had any form of starter. And I'm proved right.

Gear layout on the bike has been great today, with valuables in the rucksack permanently on my back, low value stuff in the holdall strapped across the pillion seat behind me, and clothing in the two pannier bags. This arrangement seems well balanced and saves time unstrapping the rucksack every time I want to leave the bike for more than a few minutes. I feel like I'm properly in the groove now, and me and my 1450cc chariot are well and truly on our way.

Elmer Long's Bottle Tree Ranch.

21st April. 358 miles.

Flowers In Death Valley.

A truly extraordinary day. A day of extremes which surely can only be found here in America. On the one hand the punishing harshness of the natural environment in Death Valley, and on the other the triumph of man-made pleasure seeking which is Las Vegas.

I rise early and fire the engine into life by 7.00. A thirty mile blast, dead straight across a flat and featureless plain, due west on 58 to Kramer Junction, then north on 395 past a vast complex, perhaps ten square miles, of huge mirrors which are curved in order to focus the sun's heat onto water pipes which run across in front of them. A kind of solar power station I suppose. The sun may be heating those pipes, but it isn't doing a great deal for me just yet. This part of the Mojave is what is known as a 'high desert plain', and as such is very slow to warm up in the mornings! It's the first hint that my choice of clothing might not be entirely adequate.

Cresting a slight rise in the landscape, there opens up before me the most perfect image of the lonely road disappearing across the barren landscape into the far distance with hazy mountains beyond, scrubby desert to each side and a perfectly cloudless blue sky above. I park up the bike and pull out the camera, standing on the centre line to perfectly frame the shot, with a spiky Joshua tree featuring at one side. It's a photograph which later becomes my defining image of the trip, and indeed hangs framed above my desk as I write these words. It's also become the defining image of quite a few other people's less than authentic travel stories too, as a good number of blogs and websites have 'borrowed' it and claimed it to be part of their own Route 66 journeys. I sometimes wonder if I should take the trouble to write to them and point out that it isn't actually on Route 66 at all. I was even contacted by a movie director at one time, who said he wanted to use the scene in a film and wondered if I could tell him exactly where it was. I obliged, although I've no idea if the film ever came to anything.

Cutting across to the 178 just before Ridgecrest, I begin a long winding descent into the dry, dusty, and utterly immense Panamint Valley. I've never seen landscape on this scale before. Nothing even close. It's just huge, genuinely beyond words. Vast miles of desert scrub, occasionally dotted with contorted Joshua trees and the odd abandoned miners shack next to heaps of spoil. An incredibly harsh environment, a great ocean of desert framed in the far distance by mountains of ten thousand feet and more, yet made to look almost insignificant by the endless distances of the desert which I'm about to cross.

I hope they serviced the bike well.

I cast off and embark on my voyage across the sea of dry dirt and parched vegetation, the miles ticking steadily around the clock yet the distant hills seeming to move not an inch closer. I pass huge mineral extracting plants which I hadn't even noticed at first, and a couple of dead end shanty towns, presumably housing the mine workers, all the time creeping further out into the great plain flanked five miles away to each side by the snow-capped peaks.

I eventually arrive at a junction after an age of trying to soak it all in, and make a right turn onto 190 heading for the Towne Pass, which will take me from more or less sea level to 5,000 feet and back to sea level again in under 30 miles. The climb is long and steep and twisting, and punishing on the engine. I can feel the extra heat coming off the metal beneath me and hope those air cooling fins are up to the job. The road is lined at regular intervals with large green water tanks, ready and waiting to help out motorists with overheating cars and trucks. It must be a common occurrence, and I suppose the breakdown services are never too keen to be called all the way out here. Harley-Davidson engines aren't cooled by water though, so the only solution to overheating is to pull over and put your feet up until it cools down again, listening to the metallic 'ping ping ping' and praying that it hasn't seized. I consider the idea that a temperature gauge might be a useful additional to the bike's equipment, but then again it would only provide something else to worry about.

I take my time and make the top of the pass comfortably, stopping only long enough to realise how damned cold it is up here. What I can see ahead of me now, and a long long way below, sends a distinct shiver of nervousness through me. It's Death Valley. And it looks barren and hostile, very much giving me the impression that it's going to live up to its name.

Dropping down into the intense dry heat, my nerves aren't calming. I can feel the burning sensation in my throat as I breathe in. Not surprisingly, I've never actually tried sucking on the business end of a hot hairdryer, but this is probably what it would feel like. This really does feel like a very harsh environment. I pull up at the first piece of civilisation, Stovepipe Wells, for much needed fuel. There's a small hotel built in the 'wild west' style of architecture, a little shop and a café, and not a drop of fuel. They've run out, and the next fuel is a good twenty miles further down the valley, which doesn't help the nerves. I read a story recently about a biker who stopped at the side of a road and walked out into the desert far enough to lose sight of the bike in the heat haze, just so he could fully appreciate the true isolation of the place. On turning around he found he'd lost his bearings a little, and although he arrived back at the road before too long, he was far enough away from his starting point that he couldn't see the bike. His water was on the bike. So he had a 50/50 choice. One way would lead him to the bike and a quick route out of the blistering heat. And the other wasn't good.

I set off down the valley, out of Stovepipe Wells and past a great expanse of huge sand dunes – apparently the wind funnels between the parallel mountain ranges, picking up and carrying the sand with it until the mountains disperse at the head of the valley, causing the wind speed to drop as the funnel effect is lost, and so dropping the grains of sand again to form these dunes.

I'm relieved to find that I'm far from alone now, as quite a few bikers are passing en route to that rally at Laughlin, all friendly and waving, and helping to calm my very real fear of running out of fuel and being left helpless in the blistering heat beside an empty desert highway. Thankfully the next potential fuel stop soon appears and is fully stocked, so both the bike and I top up on much needed liquids.

The ride down the valley, 90 miles in all, provides a relentless slideshow of how nature can get just too extreme sometimes, and in the process lose its beauty. Names like Furnace Creek, Badwater Basin and Dante's View don't get awarded for no reason. A burning hot, parched dry, and poisonous landscape of barren rocks, salt flats and sulphurous water, all the time dominated by the spectacular backdrop of Telescope Peak,

11,000 feet of bare rock, crowned in snow.

And yet, despite all of this desolation, flowers grow. Apparently this phenomenon only occurs once in every hundred years or so, but they are here now. Spindly and clearly struggling for water, but nonetheless draping a vast yellow carpet across most of this wilderness, with patches of a lovely vivid purple colour too, just for added effect. So how do they ever get here? Well I'm told it's all down to bird shit. The birds eat the seeds in verdant areas and then 'deposit' them in mid-flight, some falling on lush ground to flower the very next spring, and others falling in the barren wastelands of Death Valley to lie dormant but patiently waiting for decades, until an unusually wet spring brings rain and germination to the valley. I've picked one of those rare years to travel through it.

At Badwater Basin, 282 feet below sea level and the lowest point in America, I pull over and stroll down to the salt crusted surface of the dry and sulphurous lake where a few other folk are milling around and gazing at this most extraordinary landscape. The intense dry heat means it's not a place to linger too long, and a few scorching miles later I'm leaving Death Valley behind as I climb once again into cooler and fresher air towards the little community of Shoshone. I grab the opportunity to top up the tank (once bitten, twice shy) and enjoy a chat with a bunch of bikers over a sandwich and a deliciously cold drink.

Still further endlessly straight road scenes disappear into the haze while the bike and I, now very much a relaxed and familiar duo, eat the miles with the relentless reliable rumble of the engine and the gentle rush of the wind around my helmet, the dry dust of the desert in my mouth and nose, and my vision filled from all angles by massive barren landscapes which no one who has not visited this place can possibly even imagine.

I cross the state line from California into Nevada shortly before the comically named and dreadfully dull sprawl of Pahrump which, for some reason unknown to me at least, appears to be the fireworks capital of Nevada. The roadside here is lined with endless advertising hoardings, extreme in their size and ugliness and incongruity, all promoting various brands of fireworks. I wonder why?

I don't have a pressing need to stock up on fireworks, and there appears to be nothing else worth stopping for in Pahrump, so I don't. My whole body is weary and aching by now, fingers and forearms set like steel and clinging to the grips with grim determination, and I'm glad of the wider and better surfaced road for the final blast of sixty miles or so through the vast expanses of the Nevada desert towards Las Vegas.

The outskirts are dull, ugly, flat and dusty. Then suddenly, without warning of any kind, it's as if somebody has flicked a switch and there I am, cruising up 'The Strip' on a Harley-Davidson, cool as you like, singing Viva Las Vegas at the top of my voice through the helmet, and buzzing through and through, totally oblivious to the numbing fatigue from 360 miles riding through tough and hot and dusty terrain. This is just bloody amazing, once in a lifetime stuff. Not many people get to do this, but they should, and probably would if only they knew what it felt like.

The sudden transformation is bizarre. One minute it's wide open desert road and nothing but scrub in every direction, the only highlight being the glimpses to the north of the rich terracotta shades of the Red Rock Canyon national park; and the next moment I'm engulfed in this extraordinary artificial creation of colours and shapes and lights, countless thousands of lights, which don't so much assault the senses as comprehensively kick the living daylights out of them.

This is the kind of place I would normally absolutely detest, and yet Las Vegas is so extremely awful that it's brilliant. Everything is done to the limit and beyond: brighter, bigger, louder, more expensive, more intense. Whichever way you measure anything, Las Vegas outdoes it. Even though The Strip is only a fraction over four miles long, it's home to fifteen of the world's 25 largest hotels, and the city as a whole boasts well over 150,000 rooms. 40 million people visit each year, and best estimates reckon they spend almost ten billion dollars just on gambling.

In daylight, it's sensational. After dark, the neon takes over and Vegas shows you what it can really do, shows you that man-made glitz and kitsch can give nature a run for its money in the mind-boggling stakes. It really is incredible. And it just never stops. The pulsating lights, the clatter and chatter of gambling, the booming of gas guzzling seven-litre engines powering limos of improbable size, and the thundering, air-shattering explosions of straight-through pipes on hundreds of customised Harleys unleashed on the eardrums by every green light.

It's all here. The MGM Grand, Ceasars Palace, the Bellagio. Paris-Las Vegas has a full sized copy of the Eiffel Tower out in front. New York New York has a rollercoaster on the roof. And there in front of me, right on The Strip, pretty much in the middle, is a budget Travelodge. With secure parking. And vacancies. Oh yes, this'll do me just fine. $49 dollars for the night. Thursday. I book in for two nights, and Friday is going to cost me $126. That's Las Vegas for you.

The desk clerk glances at my helmet, which after a long day of hot and still conditions is sporting the kind of insect collection which you'd be impressed to find in a national museum. 'Looks like y'all been through Bug Central sir'. It does indeed look very much that way.

I'm blown away by today. I flop backwards onto the bed and think back through it. The riding has been absolutely exhilarating, the sense of pure adventure completely off the scale, and my body seems to be getting used to it now. It always does seem to take me three or four days to get past the aches and pains on a bike trip like this. I've really started feeling attached to the bike too. Dyna Wide Glides are amazing machines, the coolest design of them all for sure; and Harleys really are designed for these roads, with their endlessly long straights and long, smooth, sweeping curves. The bike's weight and long wheelbase make it absolutely perfect. Solid, stable, and just built to cruise all day, mile after mile after mile. 'Evolution' is a word which springs to mind.

I'm more than ready for the hot bath that's running, and by the time I've soaked away some of the stiffness I can feel exhaustion setting in with a vengeance. I drag myself back out onto the Strip, but only as far as the nearest decent looking bar and restaurant. I order the smallest burger on the menu, which is still over an inch thick, down a couple of beers and that's me more or less out for the count. 360 miles in the saddle and an all-night bender in Las Vegas just aren't compatible.

22nd April. 75 miles.

Hangin' Out In Vegas.

I'm going to take it easy today, I reckon I've earned it. I'm sure my arms are an inch or two longer than they should be after yesterday, and I'm comfortably on schedule. So I start with a healthy Vegas breakfast – apple pancakes with cream and syrup, and a large coffee. And the coffee keeps getting refilled, as many times as you like, still only paying once. I like that about America, they don't shaft you just for a top up of coffee.

Suitably replenished (ok, groaning under the weight) I hop on the bike mid-morning and ride along the rest of The Strip, eyes agog at the barrage of sights as I pass Ceasars Palace again, the Belaggio with its dancing fountains, Paris-Las Vegas, The Sahara and many more. I fill the tank and head off in the general direction of Lake Mead, formed when they built the Hoover Dam and now serving the combined purposes of being the water supply and the boating centre of Las Vegas. It seems rather odd passing showrooms full of speedboats when you're surrounded by desert, but nothing is quite natural in Las Vegas, so that's ok.

The bike seems to be running a bit rough this morning, so I stop and check the oil level and clean up a few connections and generally inspect for obvious faults; but it all seems in order so I carry on and don't worry about it.

The Lake Mead Scenic Drive isn't really very scenic. No particular reason, just not an especially beautiful area. Or maybe it was the signpost on the way in that's put me off the place a little. 'No Loaded Weapons Beyond This Point'.

I hit endless traffic queues approaching the Hoover Dam – the main road runs right across the top of the dam and it's only wide enough for a single carriageway which is woefully inadequate for modern traffic volumes, so they're in the process of bypassing it with a huge new road. It's quite a feat of engineering to get it across the deep and rocky canyon below the dam, although this is as nothing compared to the phenomenal achievement of engineering which is the dam itself. It's an amazing, beautiful structure, made all the more dramatic by its rugged surroundings. It was built in the 1930's to harness the hydro-electric power of the Colorado River and to provide water for the fledgling city of Las Vegas. You'll probably have seen it in a film at some point in your life, even if you didn't know it – I believe its most recent starring role was in the James Bond film Quantum Of Solace. There's only one dam like it in the world. It's genuinely beautiful in a way which such wonders of science and human achievement often tend to be, like the world's most graceful bridges or cathedrals or even skyscrapers. And I'll tell you something else that's pretty mind-blowing too, and that's the sensation of hanging over the edge and looking right down to the bottom! I'm filled with admiration for the Americans that you can still do this, that there's no safety fence or net or officious official. Good for them.

I spend quite some time exploring the dam and the visitor centre, which is well put together and most informative and interesting. It was built during the great depression, and as soon as the proposal received the green light the little settlement of Las Vegas, then home to just 5,000 people, was immediately swamped by the arrival of around 15,000 unemployed men, all hoping to be at the head of the queue for construction work. In fact, even at its peak, the project only had jobs for around a third of them, but it was a mammoth workforce nonetheless, big enough to justify building the nearby town of Boulder City specially to house them all. A hundred men died during the building of the dam, although it's suggested that forty or so others were wrongly classified as having died of pneumonia during the process too, when in fact they were killed by carbon monoxide poisoning inside the tunnels which were dug to channel the river around the dam whilst under construction.

With the dam complete, it took six years for the newly formed Lake Mead to fill to the brim, during which time hardly a drop of water flowed out of the Colorado River delta down in the Gulf of California. Needless to say this didn't do a great deal for the ecosystem there, although the steadily increasing awareness of environmental issues has in more recent times gone some way to rectifying the damage.

Heading back to Las Vegas via the lake again, I run into yet more very heavy traffic crawling into town and conclude that I'm ready for long open roads once more. Enough of what we strangely term 'civilisation', so this will be my last night of crowds, bright lights and noise for quite a while I imagine.

I see men advertising strippers for hire, cars to be won on one-armed-bandits, acres of money-losing opportunities in the gambling halls, the biggest toffee apples I've ever set eyes on, fat people, fatter still people, and yet not one instance of drunkenness or loutish behaviour. The many people I encounter and overhear as I'm wandering around soaking up the sights and sounds help to add a great deal to my growing collection of excellent American quotes, in addition to the 'Bug Central' one from the motel.

'God bless America' – yep, they really do say it. Endlessly.

'Awesome', even more endlessly.

'Y'all keep yer rubber down' – this is a bikers expression of good luck and safe travels, implying that if the rubber is 'down', then the bike is the right way up.

I've also perfected the Harley riders' 'low wave'. A very nonchalant move of the left hand out to the side and slightly downwards, usually one or two fingers extended, as if pointing to the central white lines. You can't do it in England, because we drive on the left and your right hand is always holding the throttle, so we tend to just nod instead.

I've loved Las Vegas, but I probably won't come back. For me, it feels like it should be a once in a lifetime experience. So for my last evening in this extraordinary city, I install myself in a relatively quiet corner of a restaurant and enjoy a leisurely meal and a few drinks while mulling over my first few days on this great adventure and how I actually came to be here.

As I touched on earlier, I'd spent the previous ten years working in sales and marketing for a small independent company in the conference and events industry. Like many of my colleagues, I'd worked hard and played hard and was overdue a decent break. The business had grown from nothing to become very successful and highly regarded in its field within a relatively short space of time, but cracks were beginning to show. The owners, mistakenly, put that success entirely down to their own brilliance, their swelling pride starting to suggest that a fall might be on the horizon. Promises of share issues to those like myself in the next layer down proved to be empty; and 'do as I say, not as I do', gradually started to take over from the earlier ethos of all being in it together.

When the MD returned from a lengthy sabbatical pronouncing it to be a fine idea, it provoked in me the realisation that after ten years at the coal face, that's exactly what I needed too. My own immediate boss didn't agree, however, making it very clear that 'we can't have the tail wagging the dog' around here, and I should cease having such fanciful ideas and just stick to doing what I was paid to do – bringing in the beans.

This left me, I felt, with a clear choice. Ten years is a long time in the same job, and I didn't want to stop enjoying it, I didn't want to feel myself going stale. I knew I needed a change, or at the very least some time out to take a breath and recharge. But that option wasn't on offer. The boss needed the golden goose to keep on laying, and as I'd recently taken on a new mortgage he reckoned I had no choice but to do as I was told.

He was wrong. I did indeed have a mortgage to service, but I also had a few quid spare. Not a fortune by any stretch of the imagination, but enough to ease the decision to jump from a ship which I suspected was in any case beginning to let in a little water.

And all the while that this was unfolding I was becoming more focussed on the adventure I wanted, and needed, to undertake. The one thing which was absolutely clear to me, come what may, was that I was going to travel Route 66. That much was certain, my mind was made up, and all that needed to be resolved was what, or who, was going to give way in order for it to happen. In the end it came down to a final and straightforward request for the time off, which was met with an equally final and straightforward refusal.

And so a few days later I resigned, which appeared to cause rather a shock. I can only say to those concerned that they should have listened, and they should have taken a few minutes to think it through. After all, I was only after a few weeks leave, and unpaid at that. I don't look back with ill feelings though, as it worked out well for me. The cracks in the business grew bigger, and a few years later the ship did indeed sink. It turned out that I'd picked a good time to move on in any case, but most importantly events had conspired to allow me to make the trip which undoubtedly helped to shape who I am and how I live my life today.

Others hung on to the bitter end, keeping their faith in the safety of surroundings which had served them well for so long, and were ultimately cast aside with little warning; unable to depart, as I did, on their own terms.

And that was one big life lesson for me, right there. Nothing lasts forever, and you're a fool if you let yourself believe it will. When your gut instinct starts telling you it's time to change something, then you'd better pay attention because it's probably right. Don't let the grass grow under your feet, don't let yourself become a victim, and always remember that fortune only favours the brave.

23rd April. 337 miles.

Desert Roads.

Today is the day that I think I really begin to understand just what people mean when they talk about the 'big country'. I see vistas, one after another after another, which are simply indescribably huge. Huge beyond all comparison. Huge beyond anything I can possibly imagine. I remember last summer riding across a great plain high up in the Himalayas, looking all around me in constant wonder at the vastness of it. This, the Mojave Desert, simply dwarfs it.

The day starts with a couple of hours' blast down Interstate 15 from Las Vegas almost back to Barstow, on the way climbing over the 4,730 feet high Mountain Pass (now there's an imaginative name for a mountain pass!) and across high desert plains so wide that I can ride for half an hour without the view changing, without getting perceptibly closer to the mountains in the distance ahead, or moving forwards in relation to those which stand many miles away to either side.

The ride consists of a series of 30 mile or more stretches of perfectly straight road across the scrubby plains, flanked by distant mountain ranges. Then the road rises over the crest of a low ridge to reveal the same thing all over again, and again, repeating seemingly endlessly. I can't help but keep thinking of the wonderful old Clint Eastwood film High Plains Drifter. Now I really understand what these 'high plains' are – vast deserts, yet you're at perhaps three or four thousand feet above sea level. Imagine what it must have been like a hundred and fifty years ago, having to cross this lot on a horse! And, I suspect, without even the aid of a nice smooth straight ribbon of tarmac or the Collins Road Map of the USA.

I eventually re-join Route 66 at the virtually non-existent township of Minneola; and a few miles along an absolutely perfect stretch of old original road, complete with the '66' symbol inside a shield stencilled neatly onto the tarmac, I stop for what turns out to be a lengthy coffee break at the delightful Bagdad Café, where they shot the film of the same name – which is also delightful, if more than a little quirky.

Here I meet the first of the great characters of old Route 66 in the form of the charming lady hostess, Andrea Pruett. She's the kind of wholesome character who is instantly likeable, with a permanent smile and kind blue eyes beneath a bouncy bundle of wavy blonde hair; and an inexhaustible supply of friendly conversation and genuine interest in everyone who visits. The café's been in her family for many years, and Andrea seems to be the last survivor and left holding the baby. But resolutely, and unfailingly cheerfully, year after year she keeps the place more or less in one piece, surviving partly on passing travellers like myself with too much time on their hands, but mainly on a reliable stream of around five coach parties per week on an assortment of Route 66 sightseeing tours, and even the occasional bus full of cult film fanatics.

As if to underline the point, a coachload of Spanish tourists rolls onto the forecourt as we're chatting away and out they pour, cameras a-clicking. Andrea dutifully slips into a series of well-rehearsed poses – behind the counter as featured in the film, in front of the old juke box as featured in the film, sitting on the shiny plastic seating as featured in the film, and so on, as featured in the film. I'm impressed at the way she still does it with warm enthusiasm, and must keep it up day in day out. She really is just one of those bright, cheerful, happy people who always brighten up your day. Good for her.

Andrea is the first of many people who will show me that if you stop in the small places you get to have a good chat with the locals and the characters who make your trip special and always add something to your life. And if you just stop in the larger places, the places owned by big business and run by people on wages, then nobody cares who you are or what you're doing; you're just another tourist with a wallet that needs emptying.

The coach soon rounds up its cargo and presses on with its schedule. I drink more coffee and chat with Andrea, mainly about the old times. Not much else happens or seems likely to. You can just about hear the traffic on the Interstate a couple of miles away, and watch the constant flow of passing trade which once was Andrea's, but no more. She's doing the impossible every day here, surviving despite the almost complete loss of the one commodity which caused her business to be here in the first place – travellers on Route 66. Back then it was a busy road. The journey itself, along with all the special people and places along the way, was as much fun as reaching the destination, and people like Andrea were a big part of what made it special, of what made it so enjoyable.

America really did get its kicks on Route 66, but then somewhere along the way we all got impatient and bored with travelling for the sake of the journey. The destination became the sole focus, and we built the multi-lane interstates to help us get there quicker. Before we knew it, the character of the road and an entire way of life had gone. Well, almost gone. People like Andrea hang on to it and keep it alive, and we owe a great debt of gratitude to her and her tribe.

A fabulous, perfect, as-imagined-in-the-movies classic piece of Route 66 riding follows through Ludlow, past huge lava fields of black contorted rock which really does look like it was boiled furiously and then cooled to become solid again before all the bubbles had smoothed out. The lava flanks the road for miles before the source reveals itself as the long extinct volcano now known, not as the mountain it once was, but as the Amboy Crater.

And so to the closed and boarded up, but allegedly soon to reopen, Roy's Motel. A rather faded handwritten sign informs the passing traveller that not just the site of the motel, but in fact the entire town (that adds three more buildings to the total) has been purchased by a businessman who 'hopes to restore it to its former glory'. I can only think that the man has a lot of work to do. Here I actually see a fully authentic piece of tumbleweed come rolling and bouncing across the dusty forecourt on a little gust of wind and blown dirt, just like in some old western film.

A mile further up the road I really need to stop for a toilet break. I park up on the verge and walk a few paces into the scrub so as to reveal myself to a small bush rather than the truck driver who I can see approaching in the distance. As I return to the bike, a familiar deep rumble announces the presence of another Harley. The rider slows to a snail's pace, and through the deft use of a variety of hand signals we conduct a brief conversation:

'Is your bike ok?'

'Yeah sure, no problem, just stopped for a pee'.

'No worries dude, y'all have a nice day, keep yer rubber down'.

'Thanks mate, you too'.

Clever things, hand signals. This kind of exchange happens all the time, and it's not just an American thing, it's a biker thing. I, like many people I'm sure, was brought up with a good old traditional stereotype of the biker as being some kind of semi-domesticated being, leather clad and stinking, mainly of the carcasses of dead vermin from which he had recently bitten the heads, unlikely to have ever held down a job or paid any tax, and almost certain to murder you upon sight. Thankfully the truth is rather different. The bits about leather and tending to smell a little are frequently true, but I know of no other fraternity which maintains such a powerful code of caring and inclusion. A deadbeat drifter and a provincial solicitor share not one single thing in common, until they each own motorbikes; whereupon they instantly acquire an unbreakable mutual respect and will do anything to help each other out of a scrape.

Owning a bike, and as a result being so frequently approached by complete strangers who just want to check if everything's ok, has profoundly changed my view of human nature. I grew up rather untrusting of strangers and those who were 'different', and my mind broadened later than most; but bikers have without doubt opened up entirely new thinking for me on the subject of human nature, caring, and kindness toward strangers. How often does a car driver ever slow down to check another is alright?

Back on the bike, and the big country keeps on being big with yet more of those road-disappearing-into-the-distance experiences coming one after another. Three stretches of long straight road, each clocking up at more than twenty five miles, with just a slight crest and a bend of no more than a few degrees between one and the next, leading me steadily onwards through the mighty Mojave Desert, and a whole lot more easily and comfortably than those desperate refugees of the 1930's – that journey must have been sheer hell in the heat of summer, in broken old jalopies, and on unmade roads.

The scenery, though absolutely marvellous, is nonetheless in danger of becoming monotonous, and so it's a pleasure to welcome another fellow traveller alongside me during this stretch. Moving sometimes very close, sometimes a mile or two away across the desert, and sometimes providing a little excitement with a race for a few miles, the Santa Fe Railroad is going to keep me fairly constant company for much of the next few hundred miles.

In many places across America it can be hard to find the original old Route 66, buried as it often is beneath urban expansion or new road building. But for the keen tarmac detective there are always two very helpful clues as to its whereabouts. One is the railroad, which originally ran parallel and close to the road along much of its length, and of course is also more likely to remain on its original alignment to the present day. And the other clue, should you ever be faced with two possible roads and wish to know which is the original, is the line of weathered old telegraph poles which will invariably stand alongside the old road.

The road now passes underneath its soulless modern replacement, Interstate 40, and into the town of Fenner, consisting of little more than a petrol station which it must be said I reach with some considerable relief. I really don't know what had possessed me to pass up the previous chance of topping up the tank. I can only imagine some sort of madness had passed through my mind right at the crucial moment. 'Here I am in the middle of a bloody enormous desert, I have about 150 miles worth of fuel in my tank, and it would appear from the map that it's at least, oh let me see, about 150 miles to the next likely fuel stop, and there's a fuel station right there in front of me. What shall I do I wonder? I know, I'll carry on and risk running out'. Brilliant idea. Big lesson learned. The same one I learned back in Death Valley, but clearly have already forgotten.

Anyway, I've got away with it by the skin of my teeth and the few petrol fumes still wafting around my tank, so I pull up and with much relief pump just over four gallons of petrol into my, um, four gallon tank, whilst a couple of old hicks look on, swearing and spitting in turns. They're wearing oily dungarees, red and white spotted neckerchiefs, and battered Stetsons too. Very authentic.

Next comes the ghost town of Goffs, another sad victim of bypassing by the new road. The last resident clearly packed up, turned out the lights, and moved on a few years previously; and all that remains is the derelict old general store, paint peeling and shutters clattering on broken hinges, and more tumbleweed. It's worth a stop for an atmospheric photo, and if you ever find yourself filming a Western and in need of a readymade set, look no further.

I notice from the map that I'm quite close to the town of Laughlin now, where the bikers from Santa Monica were heading, and there's a steadily increasing number of bikes everywhere out on their 'ride outs' from the town before returning in the evening to drink beer and behead chickens and party through the night. Actually, they're not all staying in Laughlin, because Laughlin isn't big enough; and this is now going to cause me some problems because it's been a long day and I'd like a bed pretty soon, and every bed in the area appears to be booked up.

I decide there's some logic in riding for a little way in the exact opposite direction to Laughlin, and another brief stop to consult the map seems to suggest the rather grandly named Lake Havasu City, so that's where I head off to; passing the impressive and very appropriately named Needles mountains along the way, forming as they do a very needly backdrop to the equally appropriately named town of Needles.

I'm very very hot and very very sticky as I approach the outskirts of Lake Havasu City. It's humid as hell and getting pretty unpleasant inside my jacket, so it's a relief that accommodation is swiftly located in the form of a tidy little motel close to the centre of town which is equipped with one very welcome bonus feature – a swimming pool. Two minutes after locking up the bike I'm diving into the lovely cool water. I don't care if the surface is littered with dead insects, which it is, or that the pool is charmingly located in the middle of the car park. It's cool and fresh and feels wonderful.

Now Lake Havasu City is a rather intriguing place. In the early 1960's Robert P McCulloch bought up around 16,000 acres of barren land on the east bank of Lake Havasu on the Colorado River, with the idea of creating from scratch a kind of community cum resort dedicated to active fun and leisure. As the development progressed, McCulloch felt it needed some kind of unique centrepiece to help attract more attention and so boost property sales. And when, in 1967, the City of London decided it was time to dismantle and replace the original London Bridge, he spotted his opportunity. McCulloch bought the bridge, had every single stone carefully and individually numbered, and shipped the whole lot to Lake Havasu City where it was rebuilt stone by stone, lamp post by lamp post, and palm tree by palm tree. You'll note that one of those elements may not be strictly original.

Rumour has it that he actually thought he'd bought the much more iconic Tower Bridge and was a little bit disappointed when this one came out of the box, as it were. But anyway, they've done a jolly good job of putting it all back together, although they made it easier for themselves by initially building it on completely dry land and then digging a river underneath it to give it a sense of purpose; and it doesn't look quite right with the Stars and Stripes fluttering alternately with the Union Flags and a backdrop of desert. And there's those palm trees too, I'm sure the original architect never envisaged those being part of the scene.

Still, it's achieved its purpose of bringing an interesting, if somewhat incongruous, focal point to an otherwise remarkably dull town.

Another very authentic feature of Old London Town is recreated for me a little later in the evening, not long after I've painstakingly cleaned the bike. Here on the border of California and Arizona, both known for being largely deserts, it suddenly rains, and very heavily.

Thankfully it doesn't last for long though, and I'm soon able to enjoy a beer sitting on a terrace overlooking the imported bridge as it majestically spans the fake river, and listen to the booming engines of the fleet of pleasure boats which pass constantly to and fro beneath its two main arches. This is America and size is everything, especially when it comes to engines, and even more especially when it comes to boat engines it seems. In London they happily chugged back and forth beneath this bridge for over a century, but in Lake Havasu City they blast out the deep growling roar of a great many cubic litres of fuel guzzling monster as they thunder up the man-made river that goes nowhere in particular.

More than a little road weary, and with another amazing day to reflect upon, I'm soon in bed and pleasantly relaxed. Although not before a vigorous bout of sock washing.

Roy's Motel, Amboy.

24th April. 279 miles.

Blokes From Barnsley.

I get myself organised and loaded up after writing a few postcards home, and I'm at the post office buying stamps just after 9.00. After a brief chat with a couple of bikers (yep, more of the Laughlin crowd) I'm heading back to join Route 66 again where it crosses the Colorado River at Topock. The Colorado doubles as the border between California and Arizona, so this is the point where I finally bid farewell to California.

Immediately after Topock, something very strange and unexpected happens to the road. It stops being straight! Real curves and sweeping bends, some of them almost describable as 'tight'. It takes me quite by surprise to begin with, causing a couple of nervous wobbles, but a few bends in and I'm soon showing the Americans how it's done. And that's really saying something, because I'm rubbish at bends. But being English, I do at least know what they are, and have a reasonable understanding about how to tackle them; whereas they're such a rare thing to come across in much of America that, judging by the overly hesitant speed and woeful road positioning that every bike I encounter demonstrates, they clearly don't bother teaching you how to do it over here.

I've never been the best rider on the road before, and I certainly won't ever be again, so I make a point of enjoying this brief feeling of smugness. I'm on a hired bike which therefore has a US license plate after all, so nobody knows I've cheated and learned this skill through necessity on foreign roads. They just think I'm like them, but infinitely more talented. It's a great shame though, because there's something incredibly satisfying and exhilarating about riding a bend well and at a decent pace. It brings the machine to life somehow, and the rider too. It's a visceral feeling, the result of performing a skill with a degree of elegance, and many of these folk are probably never going to feel it.

The road leads me across the Colorado flood plain before starting to climb gently into beautiful hills which rise towards steep mounds of scree topped with huge pinnacles of bare rock thrusting skywards. Occasional glimpses of weathered wooden shacks marking long-abandoned mine entrances give a clue that there's gold in them there hills – or rather there was, or at least someone thought there might be. In actual fact they were right, very right indeed, to the tune of about $10 million which, back in 1915 when they hit lucky, was a fairly pretty penny and certainly more than enough to drive the ensuing gold rush.

Another sweeping bend reveals the spectacularly authentic looking Wild West town of Oatman, with its old weather worn wooden buildings complete with boardwalks and rails to tie your horse to. And hundreds of shiny custom bikes on a day out from Laughlin. There's some seriously smart looking paintwork and chrome on display as I wander up the single street, rows and rows of Harleys lining both sides, looking more than a little incongruous in this tiny rickety town which appears to have barely changed since it was built in a hurry after they unearthed that rich seam of gold all those years ago.

The biker bustle and banter is interrupted by a rather portly gentleman dressed in full cowboy regalia, who announces with the aid of a megaphone that the street will shortly be closed for a little while to allow the re-enactment of a Wild West shoot out, all for the entertainment of a coach load of English tourists who are presumably facing the rigours of Route 66 in air conditioned luxury. I take up a good vantage point, leaning against a post on one of the boardwalks. I think this is going to be quite entertaining!

Well the tourists get precisely what they deserve – a badly hammed-up excuse for a performance by some fat old men in silly hats, a couple of rounds of blank ammunition, and some terribly unconvincing falling over in the street. Nonetheless, it's all duly captured on a hundred camcorders, and acknowledged with a polite round of applause as the dead and wounded are helped back to their feet and dusted off ready to fight another day.

The crowd disperses via the portable toilets and a handful of hastily arranged retail opportunities, and are soon back aboard the coach and pushing onwards once more into the uncharted wilderness. I smile as I down a cold beer in a reasonably convincing saloon bar. I actually rather like this little place. But I too must press on, first over the Sitgreaves Pass and past more remnants of long forgotten gold mining activity, before descending again and leaving the hills to cross wide plains to Kingman – a pleasant looking town which makes the most of its Route 66 heritage, clearly evidenced by the innumerable 'Famous Old Route 66 Diners / Motels / Gas Stations / Barbers Shops…'. It seems there's actually very little in Kingman which isn't either old or famous, usually both.

The road onwards from Kingman continues relentlessly across vast plains of scrub and sand, thirty mile stretches at a time, before I'm pulling up at the fabulous old gas station and general store at Hackberry; an exceptionally well preserved and unspoiled combination of authentic and original memorabilia and souvenirs.

It's just an old gas station like so many hundreds of others which lie abandoned along the route. The only difference is that this one is tidy and well kept, and still sells gas. I love the fact that, apart from stocking souvenirs instead of groceries, it seems to have been kept exactly as it was the day it was built. No gimmicks beyond the original advertising signage, no tacky modernisation, just rickety old wooden and corrugated iron buildings, old fashioned fuel pumps, and a couple of stunning classic cars and a motorbike on the forecourt. It's a great place to see, it feels good, it feels right. And it seems to be surviving ok too.

Adjacent to the general store building is Bonnie's Hot Dog Stall, where I choose myself a Polish Dog for lunch. A Polish Dog, so far as I can tell, is the same as a hot dog, except a little bit longer. Somewhat more noteworthy is the absolutely delicious home-made lemonade which I choose to wash it down with.

A bright red, huge and heavily accessorised pickup truck pulls up at the fuel pumps while I'm eating, and two blokes sporting smart new cowboy hats and shiny embroidered boots climb out.

'Hi, how you doing, that's a cracking looking truck' I observe.

'Top piece o' kit that is mate, aircon and t' bloody lot in it, goes like shit off a greased shovel an' all'.

Bloody hell, they're from Yorkshire, doing the Route 66 thing together in a rented pickup truck. It all feels a bit 'Barnsley does Brokeback Mountain', but I avoid mentioning that. They're just a couple of friendly and lively lads from the north of England having a load of laughs and an absolute blast on a brilliant trip across the States, and good on 'em for getting fully into the spirit with the outfits too.

It's been a very agreeable stop at Hackberry, and the Yorkshire lads have added their own dose of entertainment and jovial banter to it, but more relentless empty plains await. I like the plains though. They offer plenty of time and space to appreciate my surroundings, not so much to think and ponder things, more to just absorb the landscape and feel free and unchained. I notice things too. I notice how, ever so gradually, almost imperceptibly, the desert is becoming just a little greener; and, rather more quickly, the soil is becoming a very deep shade of rusty red.

The road takes an immense sweeping five mile curve to the left before skirting the southern edge of the Hualapai Indian Reserve, then on for mile after mile and past half a dozen virtually non-existent settlements before closing in again on its replacement and nemesis, Interstate 40, as we arrive in Seligman. No investigation is required to discover what Seligman's claim to fame is, as the place is screaming it at me everywhere I look. It's the 'birthplace' of Route 66, and the hometown of its 'inventor'. It also looks like it's home to the most tacky, dreadfully overdone, and utterly tasteless Route 66 Visitor Centre which you could possibly imagine.

Further delving makes a little more sense of this birthplace claim – it's where *historic* Route 66 was born, in as much as the people of Seligman were instrumental in campaigning, in the late 1980's, to have the old road officially recognised as an 'historic highway' by the State of Arizona. It certainly seems to have helped persuade a few tourists to stop and spend some dollars in a town which otherwise doesn't have a great deal to shout about. Something which really makes the place stand out to me though, and no thanks at all to the good folk of Seligman, is the sight of snow – and this time it isn't several miles away and eleven thousand feet above me. It's far too close for comfort!

Beyond Seligman, I'm running more or less parallel with the new road as I pass through Ash Fork and Pine Springs before leaving Route 66 at the town of Williams and heading due north. My first detour from the main route, to Death Valley and Las Vegas, was nothing short of an amazing experience; but I'm even more excited about this one. Truth be told, I'm actually shivering; but unfortunately this isn't due to my intense feeling of anticipation about what lies about sixty miles further up this road. No, I'm shivering because I'm absolutely bloody freezing. I've hardly noticed it until now, but the temperature has been steadily dropping throughout the day, and for these last few miles of the afternoon it's made worse by the fact that I've started riding through light rain showers. Not enough to get particularly wet, but more than sufficient to kill off any chance of keeping warm.

Of course I've seen pictures of the Grand Canyon, who hasn't? But there are some sights in this world which cannot be adequately captured by photographs, whose sheer majesty defies the limitations of artificial imagery, and the moment its vastness opens up before me I know that this is the most extreme example of them all. As I cover the last few miles approaching the canyon, the landscape offers not a single clue that it's there. Really, if it wasn't for the signposts, you wouldn't know until the moment you arrived right on the very lip – or, I should say, the 'rim' as it's known.

The road stops right at the edge. I pull over and park up the bike, dig out the camera, and within twenty paces I'm standing before the greatest natural phenomenon on earth. It's utterly mind blowing, I can't take it in, I just can't. My jaw drops. I'm simultaneously thinking 'oh my god, it's incredible' and 'I need a hot shower very soon indeed'. I'm so cold, right to my core, I can't actually hold the camera still enough to get a shot in focus. I take a few, only to be deleted later and re-taken in the morning. I'm in a muddle, it all seems blurred and confused. I'm gazing at the most extraordinary sight I've ever seen, probably ever will see, but the cold and shivering has completely taken over and my mind doesn't really know what's going on. I need to sort this out, and quickly.

Back on the bike, shaking uncontrollably, I ride another mile along the road. There are plenty of tourist hotels here, but of course they're all booked up solid and I really need warmth, quickly. But it's ok, luck sets in just before panic and the next thing I'm consciously aware of is that I've got myself an overpriced but very lovely and spacious room, and my window is twenty feet from the canyon rim. And I have a shower. A warm shower. I stand beneath the stream of water for ages, slowly thawing out, feeling that tingling pain as my fingers come back to life, feeling the shivers subside and transform into a comfortable warmth inside as well as out. Bloody hell I really was cold back there, and it crept in so gradually I didn't notice. I'm going to need to watch out for that in future, because that's exactly how hypothermia gets you.

A good warm through and an hours rest, continually staring out of the window and pinching myself, is that *real*, and I've got some energy back in my body and mind. I'm excited. And hungry, extremely hungry indeed, it's been a good long day, and a couple of beers wouldn't go amiss either.

America's most clueless maitre d' is making a hopeless hash of getting people seated. Dithering is his specialist subject, and he's turned it into an art form. The restaurant is less than half full, yet despite the innumerable opportunities to get people seated and ordering, we're all being held in a lengthy queue which isn't advancing at all. I get chatting with a very charming and friendly couple who are patiently standing immediately in front of me. Wally and Marilyn are in the hospitality business themselves, so are also marvelling at the maitre d's incompetence. We've more or less exchanged our full life stories by the time it's our turn to be slotted into one of the sea of available tables, and they invite me to join them. We all agree that, having waited so long, we're actually beginning to lose our appetites a little, and so decline yet another invitation to indulge in the Super Salad. Another wise decision, as the steak which we've treated ourselves to is huge. It's also delicious and perfectly cooked, and my new friends are interesting and interested in equal measure. I end up with an invitation to visit them in Michigan when I pass by.

Back in my room relatively early, there's no phone signal and I'm itching to share where I am and what I can see right outside my window. I put my feet up on the bed with a drink and pull out the guidebooks to learn a little more about this place. The first thing that really leaps off the page at me is the altitude. I'm seven thousand feet above sea level, so no wonder it's bloody cold! I'd never realised. I've been riding along across endless miles of what is basically desert, and it just doesn't occur to me that desert can be at such a high altitude. Rather stupid of me I suppose, because I know full well that the Grand Canyon is a mile deep, and the end of the canyon is nowhere near sea level, so of course it's got to be well over a mile high here.

I can't wait to explore properly in the morning, and I shall certainly wrap up warm.

25th April. 209 miles.

The Grand Canyon.

It must surely be nature's greatest triumph, it has to be. Some six million years of intricate, painstaking work by the elements have created a masterpiece of such immense majesty that it is impossible to imagine there could be anything more beautiful, anywhere.

I'm awake at 6.30 just as sunlight is starting to stream through the gaps between the curtains. In and out of the shower as fast as possible and I'm out walking along the 'rim trail' westwards from Bright Angel Lodge just before 7.00.

It's clear and sunny, but with a biting chilly wind; and looking down into the canyon there's a thin haze blurring the definition of the myriad rock features. I'm generally a little hazy myself first thing in the morning, but these bright and cold conditions and the mind-blowing sight before me make it impossible to be anything other than wide awake and acutely aware, fully tuned into the intensely powerful experience I'm enjoying.

The sun is climbing and warming all the time, and the air in the canyon below me is rapidly becoming clearer, the definition sharpening, the effects of light on the rocks becoming more dramatic by the second. I'm staggered. It's breathtaking.

No one else has bothered to make such an early start, so I have the greatest natural wonder on earth virtually to myself. The quiet serenity of it is deeply moving. The place is gargantuan in its physical scale, yet utterly peaceful and calm.

I walk for a few miles along the rim, as far as Mohave Point, simply gazing in wonder at the vistas unfolding before me and below me. Ten miles across to the north rim, one mile down to occasional glimpses of the Colorado River, still gouging the canyon ever deeper and even more incredible for the countless generations yet to see it.

Often I walk out onto a rocky viewpoint to gaze in silent awe at yet more colours, chasms, contours, cliffs and strata. Sometimes I just sit for a few minutes with my feet dangling over the edge, trying to make some sense of it. Strangely, I simply find it impossible to actually think. I just can't order and store all my thoughts and the images my eyes are seeing. I'm just here in my own world, on the edge of the Grand Canyon, and it's extraordinary.

The shadows of the clouds drifting across deep red

cliffs, green plateaux and conical mesas far below will stay with me forever. Not in any logical order, but there in my mind somewhere. I hope that the photographs will later provide a clearer framework for everything I'm seeing but failing to process here in the moment, and show me little details which I'm probably missing amongst the enormity of it all.

I arrive back at my hotel just in time for the 11.00 am check out deadline, which I have the distinct impression will be rigidly enforced, and enjoy a well-earned coffee and a pastry sitting out in the sunshine in front of a small cafe; although I have to fight off some very over-familiar squirrels in order to keep possession of the pastry.

My private Grand Canyon experience is over now, as the tourist day is winding up to optimum performance and the Japanese tour buses are arriving. Wave after wave of them, and I'm afraid to say I can't help being reminded of the attack on Pearl Harbour where they similarly overwhelmed a small part of America in vast numbers.

I set off on the bike, making my way east along the edge of the canyon. Within just a couple of miles I've escaped the main tourist hotspots and again the quiet serenity astonishes me. I pull up for a few minutes at every viewpoint to be treated to yet another fresh perspective, or to peer over a cliff face which takes my breath away.

By mid-afternoon the camera toting hoards have

caught up with me again and the canyon is no longer mine. It's time to leave, although half a dozen unexpected viewpoints still remain, just to underline the fact that the Grand Canyon, when it comes to natural wonders, truly is the big one in every sense.

One final and wonderful little surprise awaits me just a few miles down the road though. The Little Colorado Canyon, a completely vertical carved gorge dropping a thousand feet from the flat green plain to the rocky and deep red river below. Funny really; in England a feature like this would be crawling with tourists by the thousand, and gift shops and ice cream. But here, nothing; not even a car park.

Riding east towards Cameron, I feel a very welcome rise in the temperature as I gradually drop from 7,000 to 5,000 feet above sea level, although it's a rather short lived pleasure as my route south to Flagstaff takes me through snow covered mountains around the 12,000 foot Humphreys Peak.

Flagstaff is cold and wet, and not at all inviting, so I keep on riding and head east again on Interstate 40 towards Holbrook, with a little detour onto the old road through Winslow, Arizona. Yes, *the* Winslow, Arizona, as in 'Well I'm standing on a corner in Winslow, Arizona, and such a fine sight to see. It's a girl my Lord, in a flat-bed Ford, slowing down to take a look at me'. (Take It Easy by the Eagles, in case you were born a bit too late). I found the corner alright (it's actually a crossroads), but unfortunately there was no girl in a flat-bed Ford; just a rather plump lady police officer, a police car and a fire engine, all taking a fairly leisurely approach to sorting out some minor incident.

I take a further little detour to the south, rather on the spur of the moment, to have a quick look at Meteor Crater. Good grief! Something about a mile wide must have dropped out of the sky here a few thousand years ago. But where did it go? Why is only the hole left? The answer, in case you're wondering, is that the incredible force of the impact effectively vaporises the meteor, so all you can see afterwards is the crater.

Old Route 66 is mostly buried beneath Interstate 40 on this stretch, but I've still managed to find a couple of lovely old sections through the centres of Winslow and Joseph City, as well as a little earlier as I was leaving Flagstaff, and they all help to conjure up the old magic.

The afternoon is wearing on and it's time to get myself moving to Holbrook and find myself a bed. The urgency is cranked up a couple of gears more by a menacing bank of dark clouds racing across the plains towards me like a gigantic grey fist driving a chilling wind before it. The landscape is so vast in this part of the world that you can see weather systems approaching for miles. At home the weather just changes almost without warning, but here the ability to see the storm building and bearing down on me is dramatic and sends shivers right through me. Short stumpy rainbows look as if they're trying to anchor the clouds to the ground, and stinging tentacles of rain piercing down to the plains are visible at their leading edge. It looks very unpleasant back there and I really don't want to be in amongst it.

I make it to Holbrook and the fabulously quirky Wigwam Motel, (strapline 'Ever stayed in a wigwam?') just in the nick of time as the squall hits. Thankfully there's a covered awning in front of the reception building; so me, the bike and the gear all manage to escape a thorough drenching as the rain lashes down. It's fast moving and short-lived though, and by the time I've checked in and got myself a key to a wigwam the squall has already passed on its way and the sky is clearing.

I'm in one of about a dozen concrete wigwams, each with a double bed, en suite bathroom, a TV and a little table and chair; plus an old classic car or pickup truck parked outside. This is one place which really is exactly as the guidebooks promised. A night of fantastic quirkiness for 42 dollars, not bad. I've got some phone signal here too, and it's lovely to catch up with the kids again.

What a day. I feel very privileged to have lived it.

I'm tired, physically and mentally, after today's assault on my body and senses; so I just stroll a few yards down the street and slide into a corner booth in the first reasonably pleasant looking eatery. It's a kind of rustic steakhouse and bar, and not overly troubled by customers.

'Howdy' comes the rustic steakhouse style greeting from a waitress wearing a cowboy hat. 'Will you have Super Salad to start?'

'Ok, you're going to need to explain this to me please. What exactly is this Super Salad which everyone keeps trying to tempt me with?'

She looks a little puzzled. 'Well, it's just the choice of starters sir. You can have soup, or salad. Just help yourself to as much as you like from the buffet bar over there'.

I can't help laughing out loud, and have to reassure her that it's only at my own stupidity. I'm a big fan of almost any flavour of soup, and I've missed out thinking that all I was being offered was a mountain of lettuce.

Following an excellent and very large bowl of soup (no salad), I get a decent steak down me and spend an hour with the map and a couple of beers. I'm six days into my journey now, and a bit of mental arithmetic with the aid of a beermat and a borrowed pencil tells me I'm comfortably ahead of the overall rate of progress I need to achieve. It's time to slow the pace a little.

26th April. 138 miles.

A Geology Lesson.

I'm awake around 8.30 after a long and deep sleep. Parting the curtains and peering out of my wacky little wigwam, I'm greeted by sunshine and a bright blue cloudless sky. Wonderful!

I decided last night to take things a little easier for a day or two, so I resolve to begin the morning in leisurely fashion with a few more coffees than usual and a bike cleaning session. The poor thing is caked in filth from the wet roads of the previous two days, and bearing little resemblance to the gleaming vision in chrome and metallic paint on which I set off from Los Angeles.

I pinch the bucket from the ice machine in reception while no one is around and sacrifice the flannel in the bathroom to create my cleaning kit, along with a good dollop of shampoo to cut through the grease. It's a bit unconventional, but it does the job perfectly well and I can soon see my reflection again in the exhaust pipes.

With a shiny machine beneath me and a warm sun above, I set off on my way. First to the post office to send a few cards, then southeast on 180 for twenty miles before turning north into the Petrified Forest and Painted Desert national park areas – a detour highly recommended by pretty much every guidebook I've read.

The day soon turns into a fascinating kind of mobile geology lesson, stopping every couple of miles or so for a stroll amongst fantastically coloured and textured petrified tree trunks which litter the landscape all around me. These trees died and fell about 225 million years ago and were washed into an ancient river system where huge amounts of sediment quickly buried them, cutting off the supply of oxygen and thus dramatically slowing the process of decomposition. Over the ensuing millennia, minerals such as silica were gradually absorbed into the logs where they became crystallised, effectively replacing the wood as it slowly decayed, and resulting in a perfect replica of the original tree made almost entirely of quartz and with a variety of impurities like iron and carbon creating vibrant shades of red, pink, orange, white, purple, green and black. Then around 60 million years ago, movement of the tectonic plates beneath forced the landscape upwards, increasing its exposure to erosion by wind and water, and gradually revealing the now fossilised remnants of the trees. This movement also had the effect of cracking the incredibly brittle material, leaving them today looking as though they've all been neatly cut into manageable sized logs by someone using a chainsaw.

The park covers about 350 square miles in all, and there are thousands of these fossilised remains lying everywhere, from individual bits of log to entire tree trunks looking a little like oversized chopped up sausages. Souvenir hunting is clearly an issue, as numerous signs warn of the dire consequences of being caught with a couple of tons of rock in your pocket. There's even a great story about a curse befalling anyone who fails to resist the temptation, and the park rangers' office apparently regularly receives parcels containing returned bits of fossil along with letters of apology and pleas to lift the curse.

It's a fascinating place, the like of which I've never seen before, and all the better for being largely deserted today; so I spend a good amount of time wandering about exploring and taking photos and sitting on logs pondering how incredibly ancient it all feels.

A little further up the road I stop for another exploratory walk and scramble around the kaleidoscopic strata of the Blue Mesa with its layers of cream, red and blue coloured clay; its softness causing it to weather with countless little rivulets which give it an appearance quite akin to a lunar landscape. It's a weird kind of place, like a miniature mountain range painted in the most unlikely palette of colours you could possibly imagine. It's funny to think that if it was man-made, it would be dismissed and ridiculed for being so completely unrealistic.

Next on my educational sightseeing tour comes the tongue twisting Peurco Pueblo, an ancient Indian settlement dating from around 1,100 AD. I thought the Indians were all about tepees, but it seems they were more than capable of knocking up an impressive permanent structure too. This place consisted of a collection of buildings arranged in a square enclosing a huge central plaza, and extending to about a hundred different rooms, all still clearly visible so you can get a proper idea of how it once looked. I feel a powerful sense of mystery and spirituality exploring the remains of the dwellings of ancient civilisations, with their hieroglyphics carved into the rocks and still as crisp and clear as the day they were created; and I'm pleasantly surprised to find that nothing is protected by steel or glass, it's just sitting there for you to wander around, examine and photograph, and I suppose add your own little bit of artwork if you really wanted to.

Another couple of miles up the road I stop again and gaze from an elevated vantage point across the expanse of the Painted Desert, a vast area of Badlands landscape disappearing far into the distance in pastel shades of reds, oranges, whites and greens.

The Grand Canyon yesterday was a dramatic assault on the senses with its massive scale and infinite complexity, whereas today is a rather more gentle and continually changing slide show of geology, geography and history all vying to outdo each other with their interest and beauty. It's a very special, calming and relaxing place to spend some time; the sort of place where those of a particularly spiritual nature could easily get stuck for ages.

Thoroughly inspired and educated, I conclude my leisurely detour as I re-join Interstate 40 for an easy forty mile cruise to Lupton where the old road re-appears from beneath the new and delivers wonderful riding and scenery as I cross into New Mexico, passing towering pale sandy cliffs and strangely shaped rock formations all around. Cheap and tacky looking 'authentic' Indian souvenir shops and the garish roadside advertising hoardings which announce their presence are quite abundant here and do nothing for either the scenery or the perception of the modern day Indians in American society. I'll dwell a little more on that subject soon.

I arrive in the town of Gallup just ahead of a sharp hailstorm. Gallup is a run-down dump of a town with nothing going for it. In fact the only highlight is that I'm able to find a hotel with free internet access and get a few emails sent off to family and friends.

Fine dining establishments aren't in abundance here either, and I end up getting my first experience of the Taco Bell chain – a kind of Mexican McDonald's. To my surprise the offering is reasonably palatable, although I shudder to think what it actually contains. Fast food is monopolising the news reports whenever

I turn on a TV this week as it happens, thanks to the shocking story of Anna Ayala who claims to have found a severed human finger in her bowl of chilli at the San Jose branch of Wendy's. The restaurant chain are quite sure the finger doesn't belong to one of their employees, and logic tells me there would indeed be a fairly straightforward means of checking this, and neither does it originate from any of their suppliers. Furthermore, the county health officials have declared that the current state of the finger is not consistent with having been cooked at 170 degrees for three hours or so in amongst whatever else is contained in a Wendy's chilli. Nonetheless, the story is hitting them hard with customers staying away in droves, and they're offering a $100,000 reward for any information leading to the identity of the finger's owner.

It subsequently comes to light that Ms Ayala has significant previous form in the field of food related litigation, her daughter having reportedly received a sizeable sum in compensation a few years earlier after claiming to have been poisoned at a restaurant in Las Vegas, along with around a dozen other attempts at extortion from the likes of car dealerships and former employers; and her unlikely tale finally unravels completely when it's discovered that her husband had in fact bought the finger from its original owner, a colleague of his, after he accidentally chopped it off in an accident at work. Fast forward a few months and the saga concludes with Ms Ayala being packed off to jail and the fine reputation of the Wendy's restaurant chain duly restored.

Incredibly, Anna would go on to hit the headlines once more when, a few years later, she was sent to prison yet again after falsely reporting to police that her son had been attacked by would-be burglars outside her home and shot in the ankle. It turned out that he had in fact (yes, you guessed it) shot himself in the foot, but Ms Ayala decided to invent the story as he was on parole at the time and therefore banned from owning a firearm.

I suppose one could admire her dogged determination to keep on trying in the face of adversity; but then again, as the saying goes, 'if you keep on doing what you've always done, you'll keep on getting what you've always got'.

27th April. 164 miles.

The Uranium Burger.

I wake to a remarkable amount of noise and activity around the hotel for 7.30 in the morning, and when workmen commence tearing the reception area apart promptly at 8.00 it finally dawns on me that in entering New Mexico yesterday I had also crossed into a new time zone, so in fact it's 9 o'clock.

I dodge the workmen wielding their hammers and ripping chunks of plasterboard off the ceiling, and sit at the internet desk in the corner of reception to pick up replies to my emails. It's a little hard to concentrate as I anticipate being smacked on the head at any moment by a flying chunk of rubble, and if the dust gets much thicker I won't be able to see the screen anyway. All is well at home though, and having escaped the building a little dusty but uninjured, I'm packed and on the bike for 10.00 (real time).

Detour mode continues again today, and the route I have in mind takes me south on the 602 and then the 53 to the El Morro National Monument, before looping back to meet 66 again at Grants. One of the guide-books I have describes this part of western New Mexico as 'among the most beautiful places on the planet', which strikes me as quite a bold claim. Personally, I wouldn't go anything like that far, but the comment nonetheless provokes me into some casual pondering on the nature of beauty, and what an entirely subjective concept it is. I mean, I guess the guy wrote that because he really believed it to be the case, although of course we have no idea how much of the planet he's actually seen himself, so it's impossible to know what he's comparing it to and what he isn't. For all we know, he may never have been outside New Mexico at all. But for me, well I've seen several things on this trip already which I consider more beautiful than the scenery around me now; indeed, there are views back at home of lakes and waterfalls and coastlines which I'd say were much more beautiful. To someone else, perhaps the London skyline, or the night skies of the Sahara Desert, are the most beautiful sights of all. Beauty is in the eye of the beholder, and we're all different.

Still, leaving aside comparisons which don't really matter anyway, this route is certainly leading me through very pleasant countryside, gently undulating with the valley bottoms filled with Juniper bushes, and the slopes covered in Pinon and Ponderosa pines. The Pinons are lovely little dwarf pine trees, but with larger branches than other varieties. They only seem to grow to about fifteen feet, whereas the Ponderosas are much taller, what I'd call 'normal' pines, typically forty or fifty feet high.

Occasional escarpments of very ancient weathered sandstone, in deep reds and sandy buffs, silently witness my progress as they must have countless travellers before me and doubtless will for unimaginable ages to come. Today they're watching a happy, contented and carefree visitor; taking it easy and having a very enjoyable ride indeed.

Dominant among these rocky outcrops, El Morro is also known as Inscription Rock, and stands bold and proud above the landscape like a great watchtower. The cliff rises vertically for a couple of hundred feet, jutting out into the broad valley beneath, and around it's base are carved a great many names, dates and messages of the travellers and explorers who have crossed this land over the centuries. I particularly like the efforts of R H Orton, Capt, 1st Cal, Cav, 1866 – he had beautifully neat handwriting.

I'm amused by the irony here. If I were to kneel at the bottom of this cliff and pull out a penknife and start carving my initials and the date into the soft stone, adding my own mark to the countless others which are already here, I don't doubt that I'd soon be rounded up by the park rangers and restrained pending the arrival of the police to charge me with vandalising the vandalism. It's the same with ancient paintings on cave walls, protected and carefully preserved wherever they are found as irreplaceable artefacts; yet what is really the difference between them and the efforts of a modern day graffiti artist in any subway in any city in the world? Is it not exactly the same thing? An effort by some amateur artist to reflect their world and record it for others to see?

A very pleasant walk, aided and informed by a leaflet and map kindly loaned to me by one of the rangers, takes me all around the base and then up and along the top of the rock, adorned with wild cacti and yucca, and affording tremendous views over the New Mexico countryside. Ok that bloke and his guidebook did perhaps have something of a point.

I find that I really enjoy the occasions where I leave the bike and take off on foot for a couple of hours or so. The thing about riding a motorbike is that although it's long days of constant excitement and adventure, and it can certainly leave you more than a little weary by the time you pull up for the evening, it's not exactly physically demanding exercise is it? It doesn't matter how many times you twist your wrist turning the throttle, flex your fingers squeezing the brakes or the clutch lever, or flick the gear shift with your foot, you're basically just sitting on your backside all day doing very little at all – as clearly evidenced by the many large paunches you will invariably see squeezed into shockingly tight all-in-one leather race suits whenever you pass by a biker's meeting place. What on earth do they think they look like?

So this hike around El Morro, rather like the morning trekking along the rim of the Grand Canyon except with a climb involved too, helps to get the heart pumping and lungs working, stretches the legs, and makes me feel good.

Back at the bike and taking a quick look at the map, I see that I'm about to cross the Continental Divide, the watershed of America. Up to this point, every bit of water that I've passed has been eventually flowing out into the Pacific Ocean. And from here onwards, it all ends up in the Atlantic. Logic suggests it would be located roughly in the middle of the country, so I'm interested to see that it isn't, it's set well to the western side. It's even more extreme in South America, where on a small scale map the Divide appears to run right down the west coast – which is obvious really, because that's where the Andes are.

I keep my eyes peeled and shortly spot the sign at the side of the road – Continental Divide, Elevation 7,882 feet. Again I find the whole altitude thing hard to make sense of, as I'm riding along through countryside where it's so dry that the grass is almost permanently brown, and the landscape and vegetation looks very similar to southern Spain. At this height, surely I should be passing mountaineers planting flags on summits, not parched vegetation and sand along the roadside?

Continuing in a series of great sweeping curves, the road leads me through the extensive lava fields of the El Malpais national park, and also through a lengthy spell of very gusty cross winds which are always rather unnerving on a bike, especially when they come out of nowhere. You can adjust your balance quite easily just by leaning a little into a steady wind, but when it's hitting you hard first from one side and then suddenly from the other it can make the bike feel very unstable, as if the front wheel is about to be blown out from under you.

The road swings back northwards and the wind kindly subsides, treating me to a lovely relaxing afternoon ride in warm sunshine; with a long low escarpment of deep red sandstone to my left and wide open plains rolling away to the right, until I once again meet up with my old friend Route 66 in the town of Grants, which I instantly take a liking to.

Grants is a typical example of small-town America. It has all the usual rows of roadside motels, gas stations and cafes, some still trading and others long abandoned; but Grants is rather tidier than most places, evidence that those who live here take some pride in their town. And a big highlight for me is the fabulously named Uranium Café. It's an excellent and very friendly looking 'old road diner', with a rather bizarre decorative centrepiece in the form of the rear half of a gold coloured 1955 Chevrolet with a large basket of plastic flowers adorning the boot.

The café is owned and run by the softly spoken and instantly likeable Johnie Calahan, who sits me down at one of the fixed stools which run along the front of the counter and promptly launches into a fascinating, if somewhat elaborate, story of the café's chequered history. It's certainly seen its fair share of grand opening ceremonies. The succession of proprietors and the list of different names that it's traded under over the years must have been great business for the local sign makers. Of course this is true of so many places along Route 66, or indeed any other road for that matter. A never ending supply of budding entrepreneurs will keep on having a go at this dream or that, opening up and closing down again, often in quick succession, and from time to time something will hit the mark and stick around. This place has been a café in various guises for fifty years or so already, and it remains to be seen how long Johnie's tenure will run. He's had the café for about six years already, and being a Vietnam veteran I guess he's got some experience of battling against seemingly impossible odds.

Johnie doesn't do the typical café owner-cum-chef look. There's no generous waistline or greasy apron here, but instead a tall and slender gent dressed in tidy but casual grey jeans and blue checked shirt, with silvery thinning hair and a surprisingly un-lined face and pale blue eyes which give him a kind and gentle appearance. He's one of those people who it's almost impossible to put an age to; I'd guess somewhere in his late fifties, but I really wouldn't have a clue.

Peering through the hatchway, the kitchen appears quite 'well used', but I can't resist trying the Uranium Burger (my god, the McDonald's marketing department would have a fit). It turns out to be an excellent choice, with no trace of chemical elements contained therein, and as I tuck in Johnie continues his eloquent and strangely compelling narrative. The ups and downs, mainly downs it seems, of the café business soon drift into the troubles and the drama which seem to have dominated Johnie's personal life of late.

He recounts the saga of discovering one day that his wife had departed, shortly to be followed by a significant proportion of his life savings; and I can hear the pain in every word. It's not a rare occurrence of course, but it's the kind of thing which tends to leave you pretty wounded and right back at square one trying to figure out how to rebuild your life again. Johnie certainly deserves to come out smiling in the end, and indeed he does seem to hint a couple of times that a new love might be looming on the horizon. But it's not easy to see how this café is going to set him on the road back to financial security; I've been the only customer in the place for the last hour or so, and the few dollars I've spent here certainly aren't going to keep the wolf from the door.

Having said that, I don't think money is what makes Johnie happy in any case. It's pretty obvious that it's people that really matter to him, whether that's his family and friends or passing travellers like myself. If he can make enough to just keep rolling along day by day, then I'm sure he'll be more than content with that.

Johnie certainly ranks as one of the truly great characters of Route 66, those remarkable people who make the experience of travelling this road so special and unique. He's a genuine guy who surely deserves a lucky break at some point.

The afternoon has almost gone by the time I leave Johnie and his musings on life, love, and heartbreak; with a half-promise to return for breakfast if I find I have time. I've very much enjoyed his company, he really is one of life's true gentle souls.

Now this uranium thing – let me explain. The town of Grants, like so many others, first developed thanks to the railroad which in this particular case was constructed to transport logs from the nearby Zuni Mountains; although this industry proved relatively short lived, and the town really came to prominence in the 1930's as a result of its second incarnation as the carrot growing capital of America, and quite how or why that came about I have absolutely no idea. Then one day in 1950 a Navajo shepherd by the name of Paddy Martinez (I suspect the involvement of a promiscuous Irishman somewhere in the family history) stumbled over a lump of yellow looking rock. Uranium was discovered, and that's what Grants has remained famous for ever since.

I finish off the day by heading west on Route 66 for the first time, just to tick the box and cover the section I've missed thanks to my trip to El Morro, before returning to Grants and the Sands Motel. The Sands advertises itself as a famous Route 66 landmark but in reality it's utterly unremarkable, and strictly speaking isn't even on Route 66 as it sits half a block down a side street. Nonetheless, it's 37 dollars for a king size room, as clean as can be expected, and that's pretty good value. Still doesn't make it a famous landmark though, just saying.

Johnie Calahan at the Uranium Cafe.

28th April. 142 miles.

Two Fat Tourists.

I begin the day by furthering my education with a visit to the Grants Mining Museum, which imparts an interesting history of how the town developed through exploiting the varying fortunes of railways, carrots and uranium, since it was first established in 1880 by, not surprisingly, three Canadian brothers by the name of Grant. Well you certainly can't accuse this town of being a one trick pony.

Aside of the very well presented and informative museum, I'm also particularly intrigued by the way some visiting groups of native American Indian schoolchildren show almost as little interest in their education as their white teachers do. The museum is really great, with lots of hands-on stuff and fascinating displays which I'm certain any kid would get pretty engrossed in, and thus actually learn something from, if only the staff accompanying them would make even the slightest effort to engage with them and give them a few pointers. But they don't. It's obvious the whole exercise is regarded as a pointless and unnecessary chore; so naturally enough the kids are taking that cue, making a racket and getting up to all sorts of mischief – presumably in the certain knowledge that this will give the teachers the excuse they need to round them all up and herd them back out of the door. It's not long before that's exactly what happens.

A high cholesterol breakfast, for there is no other type of breakfast available here, back at the Uranium Café follows. It's billed, quite innocuously, as a 'breakfast sandwich', and turns out to be constructed of two very large slices of toast between which are piled two fried eggs, four rashers of bacon, and about half an inch of semi-melted cheese. It's completely impossible to eat tidily, and I don't care because it's absolutely delicious. I wash it down and allow it time to settle with a couple of coffees, and I give Johnie a set of Route 66 maps which I'm not using. They're very pretty maps but not remotely practical as travelling guides, so I hope perhaps they'll make good decorations for his café walls or just prove interesting for future visitors. I bid him farewell, knowing that I've had the pleasure of meeting a true gentleman. I hope he manages to keep the place in business and get his life back on track, because it must be a constant uphill struggle.

I'm trundling out of Grants by late morning, heading for Acoma Pueblo, aka Sky City, billed as the oldest inhabited place in America. On its own, it's a very ancient settlement with a distinctly spiritual feeling about it, constructed of adobe dwellings and perched high above the valley floor on an isolated mesa, and commanding unrivalled views across the countryside in all directions. You'd certainly see any unwanted visitors coming from miles away, and with just one steep route up through the cliffs it's a pretty easy spot to defend too. Sadly, however, it has been 'enhanced' by the arrival of modern sanitation in the form of a bright blue Portaloo (or Porda-Jaahn, as one tourist put it) plonked right in front of every house. Mind you, given that there are still quite a few permanent residents and the place has no electricity or running water, I suppose a load of ugly Portaloos is a slightly lesser evil than just chucking it over the cliffs. Why can't they at least paint the damn things to blend in a little though?

I scribble some explanatory notes in my diary: Mesa – a rocky plateau standing out above the desert, Pueblo – an ancient village, Adobe – plastered with a mixture of mud and straw, Portaloo – plastic box which looks and smells dreadful.

Unfortunately, the only way to explore Acoma Pueblo is not to explore at all, but to be herded around with a group of other tourists who collectively exemplify some of this country's most extreme examples of obesity and stupidity. I'm particularly taken aback by two gentlemen whose near identical appearance suggests that they're probably brothers. Unkempt and greasy hair which reaches almost to their waists, topped off with ridiculous cowboy hats adorned with several rather tatty feathers, and dressed in the only outfits which their extraordinary waistlines will now permit – namely dungarees constructed from enough denim to cover a tennis court.

We variously amble or waddle around the site, led by a tour guide who spouts endless rubbish in a dreary monotone which sounds for all the world like a computer-generated commentary. It's a formula which is guaranteed to disappoint. Pity.

I quietly drop off the back of the group as they turn a corner and begin to explore on my own, and it immediately becomes more enjoyable and interesting. At one point I encounter another tour guide whose concerned expression tells me he's about to correct my pioneering ways and reunite me with orderly compliance. I successfully scupper his plans by delivering a 'Hi there' with a sufficiently upbeat and assured tone that implies that all is perfectly normal here and there's no need to interfere. I leave the tourists to their terrible tours, and once I've explored enough I drop back down to the car park and the freedom of not being shepherded once again.

Albuquerque is my next destination, and I'm treated to some superb stretches of original old Route 66, along with some rather mundane ones too with the Interstate literally ten feet to the side; and stop for photos and a breather at a cracking old steel truss bridge which spans the Rio Puerco, built in the days before concrete was the answer to everything, and when even basic engineering somehow seemed to be done with more care for the aesthetic than anyone bothers with today.

On this part of the route it's very common to see sections of the very first, original road, all cracked and weed-ridden and long since abandoned, sometimes heading off and disappearing into the bushes, other times just sitting there running parallel to the new road. It seems that when they upgrade a section of road, they don't actually replace the old one but instead simply leave it alone and build a new one a few yards to one side. I guess they just don't have the pressure of limited space like we do in England. Oh and speaking of 'yards', I've noticed that they actually don't – it's always feet that distances are measured in here for some reason.

The approach to Albuquerque is terrific. I reach the edge of the plateau I've been riding on to see the whole city spread out below as the landscape slopes down towards the Rio Grande river. It's as though I'm looking down at a giant model of a city. Riding through town is a real pleasure too, with endless motels trying to lure me in with their garish neon in stylish designs and flashing colours. To me, these signs are much more than advertising from days gone by; they're an art form, and I find them both beautiful and evocative.

A casual stroll around the Old Town proves to be time well spent. It's perhaps a little over-manicured in places, but all the same a very pretty Mexican-influenced town spreading out from a central square. Good effort Albuquerque. No sign of any hot dogs or jumping frogs though – and what the hell were those song lyrics about anyway?

I'm spoiled for choice in terms of motels for the night, but to be honest I reckon they all look to be of a similar standard and price, so I don't waste much time picking and choosing.

Over dinner and a beer I ponder something I've been noticing increasingly over the last couple of days – the plight of the native American Indians. I've passed close to many Indian Reservations: the Navajo, Apache, Hopi, and Hualapai to name a few. This was their land for centuries before the early pioneers turned up and ruined the status quo, and we are all familiar with the images of proud braves astride their wild and beautiful horses, riding across the lands which have been their spiritual home for countless generations. We're also all too familiar with their inaccurate portrayal as savages who scalp, torture and murder 'innocent' settlers.

It's saddening to observe that, today, the most enterprising Indians seem to be reduced to selling cheap jewellery and woven rugs, while the rest depend on state benefits which they appear to spend almost entirely on alcohol. It's a tragic thing to see, reminiscent of the plight of many Aborigines. I'm not sure we Westerners have a great deal to be proud about in this respect, rocking up uninvited and kicking them off their land so we can settle it ourselves, and considering our behaviour to be charitable and considerate when we herd them all into little reservations which we don't mind them using, amounting to just a tiny fraction of the area of land which their forebears once freely roamed. Then when they fail to adjust successfully to the rotten life we've left them with, we look down on them with contempt and regard them as a burden on society. What are they guilty of? Just being content with the lives they led? Living in harmony with the environment and the natural world around them?

29th April. 144 miles.

Tinkertown.

It's cold again today, and by the time I've voluntarily reached an altitude of 10,000 feet it's positively freezing; in fact even colder than freezing I think, technically speaking.

I've decided to spend the first half of the day taking a detour of 80 miles or so to visit Tinkertown, before carrying on up to the Sandia Crest; both of which come highly recommended.

A quick blast for twenty miles east on Interstate 40 and I take a left turn heading steadily upwards into the hills, the landscape becoming increasingly forested as I approach my first destination.

Tinkertown is the fantastically quirky and eccentric creation of Ross Ward and his family, who over a period of more than fifty years have assembled, purely from junk, the most extraordinary Aladdin's Cave of model scenes and bizarre curios. There's a fully working circus and an entire Wild West frontier town, along with innumerable crazy sculptures, all within a ramshackle collection of buildings built largely out of old bottles set into concrete and adorned with rusting farm machinery. It occurs to me that this is what Elmer Long's Bottle Tree Ranch might be like if he'd enlisted a bit of help. Their slogan sums it up perfectly: 'We did all this while you were watching TV'. There's even an old sailing yacht, the Theodora R, originally from Maldon in Essex, which ended up here in 1991 after her owner, Fritz Damler, spent ten years sailing her right around the world and encountering all the storms, shark attacks, and other calamities one would rightly expect of such a madcap adventure. You can read all about the voyage in his book Ten Years Behind The Mast.

What I find perhaps even more extraordinary than the fact that Tinkertown exists in the first place, is that Ross never originally intended the place to be open to the public. He was creating the whole thing purely for his own amusement! But you can't keep on building this kind of place without generating a bit of interest from passers-by, and Ross eventually started letting a few folk come in to have a look around and share his hobby. One thing led to another, and in 1983 he finally gave in to the continual drip feed of curiosity and decided to open up just one room as a public attraction, welcoming a little over 900 people through the door in the first year.

Ross died in 2002, but his family continue to operate and develop the museum with annual visitor numbers now in the tens of thousands. It inspires me to think that this incredible place was never meant to be anything more than one man's indulgence of his own creative imagination and practical skills, and that the whole thing is essentially built from stuff that nobody else wanted because in their eyes it was nothing more than junk. It really does go to show that 'if you built it, they will come'.

Carrying on up the road from Tinkertown, and after countless mountain hairpin bends – as close as America gets to the kind of riding you find in the Alps – I arrive at Sandia Crest; 10,378 feet high and with an absolutely breathtaking panoramic view back across the city of Albuquerque and its perfectly geometrical grid pattern of streets and buildings. A few hundred yards along the ridge there sprouts a plethora of radio antennae, from which several local radio stations take advantage of the elevated location to beam their relentless advertising to the eager masses below.

The cold is intense at this height, with snow on the ground right at the roadside and plenty more of it falling in frequent flurries from the sky. I'm not dressed for this kind of weather, and it's a well-known fact that the Harley-Davidson motorcycle is not a great performer in winter conditions. What's needed here and now above all else is a purveyor of hot coffee. It's here alright, but just not now, as the rather tatty and dated looking café has a sign on the door informing me that it's closed for the season. I'm not sure which season they're referring to, but presumably it's the part of the year where it's not cold enough for the skiers (yes, this is actually a ski area in the winter) and not warm enough to attract a sufficient quantity of hikers and general sightseers to make it worth opening up.

This is certainly no place to be riding a motorbike in my view, so it's a hasty snapping of a few photos and a shivery dash back down the mountain in search of warmth while wincing from the extreme pain in my fingers.

Re-joining the interstate at the bottom of the hill, I head back towards Albuquerque and pull into the first roadside café which appears. It's a bit of a flea pit, but I'm not in search of salubrious surroundings – just heat. I take my time over a big mug of hot coffee, cupping it constantly in my hands during the inevitable period of sharp stinging as my fingers gradually thaw.

Back through Albuquerque, and after a little navigational confusion thanks to the cold numbing my brain, I'm heading northwards on the road for Santa Fe. It's mainly classic old 66 with an occasional stretch of Interstate thrown in, but the landscape is noticeably changing now and it's beginning to take on a much more familiar feel. Everything is a little greener and the road is lined with more English looking trees, although the architecture remains predominantly Mexican, meaning low flat-roofed buildings with their heavy roof beams jutting out beyond the plasterwork on the walls, and there remains a good deal of dusty scrubland in amongst the vegetation to remind me that I'm definitely still a very long way from home.

I'm currently following the valley of the Rio Grande river, and herein lies the reason for the increased greenery around these parts, as this once mighty waterway now finds itself classified as 'over appropriated'. This means that there are more users of its water than there is spare water flowing down it, thanks to relentless damming and irrigation projects. On its journey of almost 2,000 miles from Colorado to the Gulf of Mexico, the Rio Grande currently loses around four fifths of its water in this way, and all that change has happened since as recently as the 1950's. It's interesting to note that whilst there do exist a number of agreements between the USA and Mexico covering how they share and use the water, there's nothing more than the well intentioned efforts of a few environmental campaign groups dedicated to trying to actually do something about protecting and preserving it. We increasingly see the same pattern of behaviour around the issue of climate change, when governments the world over sign up to impressive sounding commitments which generate positive headlines and show them to be shining examples of leadership and responsibility, only to follow through by doing absolutely nothing in any practical sense and carrying on exactly as before.

Santa Fe honours my arrival with a sharp rain and hail shower, causing me to dive for cover under a conveniently placed bridge and pull on waterproofs and warmer gloves. Thanks for that! I take a quick run through the middle of town just to get the lay of the land and it looks to be a very quaint and pleasant spot, so I think I shall take a day's break here. I reckon I'm probably about a day ahead of schedule still, and I have fewer detours in mind from here on, so I'm sure I can comfortably afford the time and a proper day off is more than due.

Santa Fe is very clearly an affluent town, and I can tell without even enquiring that the downtown hotels are all well beyond my budget, especially if I'm going to be staying two nights. So I focus my search about a quarter of a mile out and soon get checked into a perfectly comfortable and conveniently located motel just a ten minute walk from the centre. It's about the least attractive building in the whole of Santa Fe, with its entire exterior decorated in an appalling combination of candy pink and cherry red, both shades presumably very carefully chosen so that the building actually clashes with itself. Thankfully they seem to have used a different designer to take care of the interior.

I get myself properly settled in, and scout around to find a reasonably well hidden corner to park the bike for its two night stay before changing into my leisure attire (same jeans, fresh shirt) and walking into town for the evening. Mexican food is, yet again, the dominant theme it seems, and there's a good choice of decent looking eateries around the main plaza, so I take pot luck and am not disappointed.

There's a noticeably relaxed air about the place and the people here. Most are tourists, so of course we're all in holiday mode and taking it easy, no rush and no stress, and as a result the conversation with the various folk I encounter and get chatting with flows easily and comfortably. I'm already enjoying my little stopover in Santa Fe.

30th April. 0 miles.

The Battle Weary Soldier.

T he railway has been a frequent travelling companion ever since I left the outskirts of Los Angeles and climbed over the Cajon Pass, and because many of the trains have 'Santa Fe' emblazoned down their sides, I'd assumed that this would be very much an old railway town, born in the days when the tracks were being laid across the wild west.

I couldn't have been more wrong. If anything, the railway was largely responsible for a significant downturn in the town's fortunes in the late 1800's; as although the railway did indeed bear its name, the pioneering engineers of the day decided it would be easier and cheaper to take a more southerly route and ended up bypassing the place altogether, leaving the once great city of Santa Fe as a bit of an isolated backwater served only by a branch line, while the rest of the west surged onwards and upwards.

Modern day Santa Fe is very much oriented towards

culture and the arts, boasting well in excess of 200 art galleries and brokers, and the centre is particularly attractive and well kept with quaint little side streets and pretty traditional Mexican architecture.

It's a lovely warm and sunny morning, perfectly suited to my plan of whiling away a relaxing day as a more typical kind of tourist. After rising relatively late and taking my time getting ready to do not very much, I walk into the main plaza again where I pick a table in the sunshine outside a café and sit down to enjoy fresh coffee and a couple of pastries, write a few postcards home, and devote an hour or so to people watching.

I spend most of the day casually exploring the older part of the town, with a spot of gift shopping and leisurely tours around some excellent art galleries. The full range is here, from very exclusive high-end galleries to street vendors with artworks of dubious provenance spread out across the pavement. It's busy yet not crowded and nobody is in a hurry, and just as I found last night there's a lovely easy going atmosphere about the town making it impossible not to unwind and go with the flow.

Towards the end of the afternoon I chance upon an unassuming but buzzing little bar called Evangelo's, just off the main square. There's a great jazz band playing and a lively convivial atmosphere throughout the place. I take up a strategic position at one end of the bar, soaking up the music and the chatter along with a couple of beers. There's an intriguing framed photograph hanging in pride of place behind the bar, and I'm sure I've seen it before somewhere; a very powerful and evocative black and white image of a battle weary soldier. It's a truly iconic portrait of an all American hero which over the years has featured everywhere from Life magazine to postage stamps, and I'm intrigued to know why it's so prominently displayed here in a little bar in downtown Santa Fe.

The bar is owned and run by Nick Klonis and, whilst I apologise to him for stereotyping here, if you've ever been on holiday to Greece, and if you picture what every single Greek restaurant owner looks like, then you know exactly what Nick looks like.

The soldier in the photograph is Nick's father, Evangelo Klonis, and he has one hell of a story. Born in 1916 on the Greek Island of Kefalonia, Evangelo was one of eight children of poor parents. Aged only 14, he left home with his elder brother and travelled to Athens to try and find work in order to help support the family, and two years later he boarded a ship bound for Los Angeles as a stowaway.

Being an illegal immigrant in the US, he had to keep his wits about him; avoiding the attention of the authorities by continually moving around and working a variety of jobs, all the while sending what he could back to help his family in Greece.

After the Japanese attack on Pearl Harbour, America entered the war and in a nationwide drive to recruit everyone they possibly could to the armed forces, American citizenship was offered to any illegal immigrant who signed up. Evangelo jumped at the chance and, shortening his name to Angelo, he joined the US Army in 1942.

He proved to be an outstanding recruit and was soon transferred to the Marines. It was during his training here that he heard the awful news that his entire family had been killed by the Nazis, and as a result he asked that he be posted to Europe to enable him to exact his own revenge on the perpetrators.

Having fought on battle fronts throughout Europe, Angelo was a highly decorated war hero by the time he received his honorary discharge at the end of the war. The biggest reward for his efforts, though, came shortly after returning home and settling in Santa Fe when he received the extraordinary news that, contrary to what he had believed for so long, his family were in fact alive and well, and in 1950 he was able to travel back to Kefalonia to be reunited with them.

He spent time both in the US and Greece, where he found himself a wife and had two sons, before eventually buying this bar and naming it Evangelo's in 1971. Angelo died in 1989, and his son Nick continues to run it to this day.

As for the photograph, well that was taken by the celebrated photojournalist W. Eugene Smith, although accounts vary wildly as to exactly when and where it was taken. It shows a tough young soldier, tired but determined, with a stubbly beard and steely piercing eyes; his helmet strap hanging nonchalantly loosened and a cigarette drooping from his lips. It's one of those pictures which is genuinely worth a thousand words. Google it and you'll see what I mean.

The rather sad end to the tale is that Angelo never actually saw the photo himself. He'd mentioned late in life to Nick that he remembered having several pictures taken by a photographer he thought might have been from Life magazine, but by the time Nick had searched far and wide and eventually tracked down the images, the remarkable man that was Evangelo Klonis had died.

I've enjoyed today, albeit it does actually feel rather strange not to be moving, and returning to the same bed for a second night in succession. It's strange how our minds and bodies object so much to a change in routine, like when you've let yourself slip into a sedentary lifestyle for too long and then you suddenly take up exercising properly again – it hurts for a while until you get used to it once more. Equally, when you're riding every day though a constantly changing land, it feels a little peculiar to suddenly have a day when the scenery stays the same.

1st May. 252 miles.

Tucumcari Tonight.

I t's my daughter Lucie's birthday today, so the day begins with a call home to chat to the kids. It's great to hear their voices and to hear all is well at home. At their home, that is. Heaven knows what state my home is in, what with builders and landscapers busy carrying out some major works that I've left them tackling in the garden, and a mountain of post doubtless piling up at the door. Still, I can't do anything about it from here, so no worries.

Lucie loved the presents which I'd left ready for her, and my son Alex is looking forward to his birthday in a couple of days' time too. Yes, they're two days, and two years, apart – read into that what you will.

Packed and loaded and back on the road, I find my way out of Santa Fe without difficulty despite some rather confusing signage to begin with. An hour later and I'm passing through Romeroville and turning south on 84 towards Santa Rosa. The landscape is again rather Mediterranean in appearance around here, reminding me somewhat of the inland mountain areas of Spain or even Cyprus. Little wonder the Spanish explorers felt so at home here all those years ago. But the hills soon open out into great broad and flat grasslands, and it's proper grass for the first time on my journey, rather than the parched and sickly looking stuff typical of the deserts and high plains. For as far as the eye can see in every direction the land is flat, a pale shade of green in colour, with the only noticeable features being the occasional barbed wire fence and of course the endless road leading ever onwards into the far distance.

I know, though, that the landscape isn't going to be my dominant memory of today. Yet again, frustratingly, it's going to be the temperature. Intense, bone chilling cold that penetrates the four layers I'm wearing along with my thick gloves, freezing me right to the very core and leaving me cruising at no more than 50 mph, just to keep the wind chill down, while I shiver and shake uncontrollably on the bike. The Weather Channel, of which for obvious reasons I'm a frequent viewer, consistently tells me it's between twenty and forty degrees (Fahrenheit) cooler than normal for this time of year. I've certainly been badly caught out in terms of the kit I brought with me; planning for warm sunshine all the way, my riding gear of choice was jeans and a leather jacket, and I'm having to pad them out with as many layers of shirts and so on that I can squeeze on beneath them, all the while thinking of my lovely warm insulated Goretex jacket and trousers hanging in the garage back at home. As every biker knows only too well, the weather is almost always either too cold, too hot, or too wet!

Oh well, no point moaning, there are things to see and places to be. I make a lunch stop at the landmark Joseph's Café in Santa Rosa, with its famous 'fat man' logo, which makes me feel better but does little to properly warm me through. Nonetheless, I refuse to let the cold spoil or curtail the day and take a very scenic run down to the historic village of Puerto de Luna, reputed to have been a frequent haunt of Billy the Kid. It's a lovely ride with the Pecos River to one side and weathered sandstone outcrops and small canyons to the other.

Back at Santa Rosa I stop to have a look at the Blue Hole, an artesian well and one of seven such holes all connected by a vast underground lake. The water is crystal clear, a vivid turquoise in colour, especially beneath the branches of an overhanging tree which shields the sunlight reflecting from the surface and greatly increases the intensity of the beautiful colour. It's something of a mecca for scuba divers, and the consistently low temperature of the water also makes it a welcome cooling-off spot – although not today thank you very much.

After the Blue Hole, I pull over at the motor museum for just long enough to discover that it's closed; although I snap a picture of its neat looking sign in the form of a bright yellow custom hot rod perched atop a thirty foot high steel column. These attention grabbing creations are starting to become a more regular feature of the roadside, and over the miles to come there are many more increasingly bizarre, garish, and just plain bonkers attempts to grab the passing motorists' attention and lure them in.

I press on towards Tucumcari along decent stretches of old road, sandwiched between the Interstate and the railway. 'Tucumcari Tonight' the advertising hoardings urge, '1,200 Rooms'. They used to say '2,000 rooms'. In truth, my guess is there are now probably little more than 500, and the majority of those remain unoccupied for most of the year. The town's decline is clearly keeping a few paces ahead of the sign writers, and it's soon evident to me that 'Tucumcari Tonight' is a piece of advice well worth ignoring; it's a one horse town whose horse has long since bolted. Just when towns like Albuquerque and Santa Fe have been getting progressively more attractive as my journey rolls onwards, with such novelties as trees and rivers and thriving businesses, along comes Tucumcari to bring me back down to earth with a bump.

Wide, flat, dull, with a five lane main street carrying absolutely no traffic, and lined with the overgrown dereliction of a thousand abandoned dreams, it feels for all the world like a town that's given up. I've been really looking forward to spending the night at the Blue Swallow Hotel, probably the most famous of all the Route 66 roadside motels if the guidebooks are anything to go by. I pull in to the courtyard, and immediately feel a strong sense that there's nothing going on here. Stuck to the glass on the inside of the front door, a hand-written notice declares the Blue Swallow to be 'temporarily closed due to family illness'. But the scrappy piece of paper announcing this fact is rather more faded and sun bleached than 'temporary' would seem to suggest.

Standing outside the closed motel and looking around me, I'm overwhelmed by that 'Oh god, what the hell am I doing here' feeling. Abandoned motels, gas stations, restaurants, and stores in every direction; the post-apocalyptic scene just occasionally interrupted by a business that's still clinging on by its final fingertip. The town was originally named Ragtown, and then Six Shooter Siding, before becoming Tucumcari, and I think both of these former monikers suit it perfectly. The town's heyday in the 50's and 60's came about primarily due to it being the only stopping off point of any size between Albuquerque, 175 miles to the west, and Amarillo which lies 115 miles to the east. Innumerable roadside businesses sprang up to feed, fuel, and accommodate the vast amount of passing trade. But of course the interstate came along and neatly skirted around the edge of the town, the distance between Albuquerque and Amarillo became much more manageable, and because Tucumcari was only ever a place you'd stop through necessity rather than because it had anything remotely attractive to offer – suddenly nobody bothered any more.

But still a dwindling few are hell bent on battling

on, seemingly oblivious to the futility of their mission to keep on drawing people to Tucumcari Tonight. It makes for a rather sad end to a difficult day; cold really lowers the spirits and saps enthusiasm, and this god-forsaken town does nothing to cheer me up with the prospect of an enjoyable evening ahead. I pull myself together, I'm not riding any further today so I'm going to have to accept my lot and make the most of it; and just a little further down the main street I find a motel that's still in business and manage to secure myself a tatty bedroom with an excellent heater. Showered and changed, with a Mexican meal inside me, I'm ready for tomorrow – and according to the Weather Channel it's going to be an even colder day; 40 degrees (that's 4 degrees centigrade) and rain with it. Keep smiling!

2nd May. 144 miles.

Snow At The Midpoint.

I'd heard rain early on in the night as I was drifting into sleep, accompanied by a strong blustery wind whistling at the window, so it's with some trepidation that I ease back the curtains after releasing the bulldog clip which has thoughtfully been provided in order to hold them tightly closed.

Fuck!

Nothing, including the bloody Weather Channel, could have prepared me for the scene before me. I'm standing, staring, jaw dropped, at three inches of snow covering the roofs, the ground, and the bike.

Desperate times require decisive action. Cometh the hour - cometh the man, and all that. So I close the curtains again, re-attach the bulldog clip, and climb back into bed. Pulling the covers tight around my chin, I stare blankly at the ceiling. It's a dream; of course, just a weird dream. I smile, and doze.

An hour later, still smiling, I roll back out of bed

again and swish the curtains aside to reveal the real scene. Bugger, so it wasn't a dream then; but the blanket of snow does at least seem to have melted to some extent. On venturing outside, though, it's immediately apparent that it's bitterly cold. The freezing air hits me like an arctic blast. It's zero degrees, and that's without wind chill. Hell, this is going to be tough.

I consider staying put for the day, but rapidly conclude that a slow death through hypothermia is infinitely preferable to an enforced stay in Tucumcari. So I wrap up as best I can, considerably better than yesterday from the outset, and gingerly set forth.

Keeping the speed right down, I use the bike's primitive thumbscrew form of cruise control (it really is just a screw which jams the throttle – not exactly safe in an emergency, but when you're on a dead straight road across the plains with a good two miles of visibility and not a car in sight I suppose it's ok) to hold the speed while allowing me to ride with one hand on the bars, and the other tucked in between my thighs for warmth. I'm surprised by how well it works; five minutes or so for each hand in turn and I seem able to make consistent progress without screaming at the pain in my fingertips. So much so, in fact, that I'm even tempted into following a long-abandoned looking section of original 66 tarmac – which after about ten minutes gives way to gravel and mud. It happens quite often; you're following part of the original road for a few miles and then without warning it just becomes a farm track, or disappears altogether into scrub and bushes. It's worth the effort though, because sometimes it doesn't end abruptly and carries right on through; real history, still alive, the same road as in the films, the songs and the folklore. On this occasion, however, it's a dead end and the only option is to turn back.

An hour and a half later, and having crossed another state line, I pull up outside the Midpoint Café in Adrian, Texas. 1,139 miles back to Los Angeles, and 1,139 miles ahead to Chicago. It's a common misconception that Route 66 crosses America from coast to coast, but it doesn't; it's essentially just a giant dogleg, diagonally from Chicago to Oklahoma City, and then horizontally across to Los Angeles and Santa Monica. About two and a half thousand miles if you take the direct route, although I'm adding a great many more with all my detours along the way.

Settling the bike onto its stand, I'm bitterly cold with numb fingers and a streaming nose; but the moment I step inside the café it's soon forgotten thanks to the immediate warmth, friendship and humour of both the host, Fran Houser, and a family of American Indians who are travelling home to Michigan from a Pow Wow they've been attending in Albuquerque. It's as pleasant a couple of hours as I've spent on the whole trip, with much joking and banter and exchanging of stories.

The café originally dates from 1928, expanding in the late 1940's and operating 24 hours a day during

Route 66's heyday. It's been through several changes of name and ownership down the years. Fran bought the place in 1990, naming it the Adrian Café, before being approached in 1995 by Tom Snyder, a travel writer and founder of the Route 66 Association, who suggested she capitalise on the significant location of the business by calling it the Midpoint Café. She wisely took his advice, transforming the Midpoint from just another roadside diner into a key staging post and must-visit attraction along the world's most famous road. Business duly improved and the increasing number of visitors started buying souvenirs as well as food and drink, and Fran had a thriving venture on her hands – showing the world that it can still be done.

A year or so later, Fran and her business are destined to become the inspiration behind Flo's V8 Café in the animated film Cars. But fame hasn't come calling yet, and despite its geographical advantage the Midpoint, just like every business battling away with varying degrees of success along this road, needs all the support it can get; so I invest in a shiny enamelled full size Route 66 sign which is going to prove a damn nuisance to get all the way home – but well worth the effort as it still adorns the back of my toilet door to this very day.

After a couple of hours of Fran's charming hospitality, she kindly snaps a few photos of me standing in the snow beside the large sign opposite the café which marks the half way point of Route 66, and wishes me well on my way towards Amarillo. I ask her 'Is this the way...' but she either doesn't get it, or perhaps more likely has just heard it too many times. Years later, I still occasionally look back at the photos which Fran took and my reaction is always the same – boy do I look cold!

The road from Adrian to Amarillo is unremarkable – this northern part of Texas, the so-called Panhandle, isn't making any effort to justify the state's brash opinion of itself – except for one absolutely marvellous example of Route 66 roadside eccentricity which appears in a field just a few yards off the highway, right before the Amarillo city limit. Cadillac Ranch. It's bloody brilliant and I love it; a straight line of ten classic Cadillac cars, each from a different era, planted nose first at a jaunty angle into the ground. It's a work of art; a weird fusion of brightly coloured junk with more than a hint of some kind of ancient burial ground or mysterious temple.

I squelch through the sticky red mud to examine closer. The cars are of course stripped of any part which will come off; they've got a base coat of yellow paint beneath countless hours of painstaking (and a good deal of not-so-painstaking) graffiti work, and there's a rough elegance in the way their tailfins reach towards the heavy leaden sky. Texas, your landscape may be utterly boring, with nothing but wide open plains growing crops and cattle, but I'll certainly admit that you can do eccentricity as well as any man can and I salute you for that.

The actual man, in this case, was Amarillo-based millionaire Stanley Marsh III, who was approached by a San Francisco based art collective known as the Ant Farm. Inspired by a children's book entitled The Look Of Cars, and particularly a section detailing the evolution of the tail fin, the Ant Farm artists' proposal was that Stanley should both provide the land and pay for the cars which would be planted in it. His suitably eccentric response was that 'It's going to take me a while to get used to the idea of the Cadillac Ranch. I'll answer you by April Fools' Day. It's such an irrelevant and silly proposition that I want to give it all my time and attention so I can make a casual judgment of it.' It seemed that they'd found themselves the perfect benefactor; a man with plenty of land, plenty of cash, and certifiably nuts!

Cadillac Ranch was first erected in 1974, and then moved a little further away from the steadily growing city in 1997. I find it quite an inspiring and thought provoking piece of art, particularly in the way that hardly any two visitors ever actually see exactly the same thing. Graffiti is actively encouraged, and so the appearance of the whole installation constantly changes. From time to time it all gets a fresh new base coat, so the canvas becomes blank again, and within a matter of just a few hours the budding artists with their spray paints start afresh.

Rinsing the claggy mud from my boots in a puddle, I'm astonished to feel that the water is distinctly warm. It would appear that the ambient ground temperature is a great deal higher than the air temperature on this unexpectedly snowy day.

I stand and take a long last admiring look at the ranch before remounting the bike and covering the short distance into Amarillo. Driving around in search of a bed, the place comes across as pretty dreary and I don't much care for it. I opt for a soulless but safe looking motel in a reasonably tidy business district just off the interstate. It has the added bonus of a large canopy in front of the entrance where I can park the bike and keep it dry, because it's looking like it's going to hammer it down any minute.

So today was the day I rode across the plains of Texas, in the snow, in May. One of those days when you've just got to grin and bear it and keep pressing on. It's all just part of the overall adventure of course – how many times have I heard, and said, that tired old line? But it's true all the same. Would I really look back on this trip as a true adventure if every day was warm, sunny, comfortable, and easy? If I never took a wrong turn, never got cold or wet, never felt the need to check the bed for insect life? If you want it easy, go on a cruise; but don't try and tell anyone it's been an adventure, because it hasn't. Pushing through the tough days and the tight spots is what makes the good days feel even better, heightens the sense of achievement and makes the whole trip all the more memorable. To my mind, it simply isn't an adventure at all if there aren't some difficult times along the way.

And yet, despite the day being dominated by snow and the cold and the mud, I still found warmth, hospitality, and friendly company thanks to the people who travel the road and those who make it their home and their livelihood.

Looking ever so cold at the Midpoint Cafe.

3rd May. 18 miles.

Dull Day In Amarillo.

U gh. Heavy, grey, leaden skies again, a forecast of cold and wet weather all day and, as previously mentioned, I'm in a town with about as much to attract me as a trip to the dentist. Nonetheless, I decide it's a day to stay put and get a few overdue chores like laundry and shopping done, so I call reception and extend my stay for a second night; and instantly feel more positive about the day. Time for a decent breakfast!

The waitress in The Waffle House is proudly sporting a lapel badge which informs me she's worked here since 1987. That's ambition for you. I indulge myself in a gallon of coffee and a couple of pints of runny syrup with a large round waffle beneath. The man on the next table has two pork chops, two fried eggs, a large cheese omelette, beans, hash browns and tomatoes. And he's not even fat. What the hell is he? Some kind of endurance athlete? He's going to need to crack off a couple of marathons to shift that lot before he starts again at lunchtime.

I get back into my room at just the right time to call my son, Alex, as today is his fifteenth birthday. He's on good form and it's great to chat again.

After tidying up a little and making a shopping list of exciting items such as deodorant, a new pen, and some beers for later, I hop on the bike and head off in search of downtown Amarillo.

If proof were needed that out of town shopping really does kill off communities, then Amarillo is it. All that seems to be left in the centre are the regional offices of half a dozen banks. No shops, no cafes, no people. The tourist information advises me that, no, I haven't simply failed to find the centre, it's just that all the shops have long since moved out to the big mall on the edge of town.

They should have got old Stanley Marsh to get more involved in running the town. Imagine what he might have created to draw in the crowds if he hadn't just limited his eccentric exploits to Cadillac Ranch? I'd have been planning to stay around for days on end, rather than just waiting for the rain to pass.

Thoroughly disappointed and taking a meandering route back towards the hotel, I do at least happen across one small independent shop – the irresistibly named Chuck's Biker Stuff. It's a warm and friendly Aladdin's Cave crammed with just about every garment, tool, gadget, and accessory that a biker could possibly need, plus an awful lot that you won't ever need but is kind of tempting all the same, and it's all amazingly cheap too. After a lengthy mooch around I buy myself a tool roll – a kind of small bag made from stiff and heavy leather, tubular in shape, which straps to the front forks and holds tools or other bits and bobs. The till receipt bears the message 'God Bless You.' It's good to support a small independent business, and it's good to see that they appreciate it.

The rain sets in properly before I've made it to back the hotel, and my feet are sodden by the time I'm parked up. Where is the sunshine and pleasant warmth that early May should be treating me to? Why this incessant cold and wet? It's really pissing me off now. I spend the rest of the afternoon cleaning clothes and doing my best to dry them on a makeshift washing line strung across the shower; improving how a few things are packed, and generally just taking stock and re-organising, accompanied by the background babble of crap on the TV.

By evening a damp, still, and depressing blanket of thick drizzly mist has enveloped the city. It feels like a dull December day in England, not like spring in Texas. They do say that Texas needed the rain, but I wish it had waited just a few days longer before arriving. Never mind, not every day can be a great day, I think I've established that beyond any doubt, and I know I'll achieve absolutely nothing whatsoever by moaning about it. It's a bit of a first world problem, isn't it?

4th May. 174 miles.

Slaughter At The Canyon.

See – it all feels so much better already! A lovely bright spring day greets me at last. Perhaps Texas isn't so dull after all? Perhaps Amarillo isn't as dreadful as I thought yesterday? Maybe it does have a buzzing downtown area, but the lady at tourist information just couldn't be bothered to direct me there? I suppose, thinking about it, places are only really dull if you allow them to be. Choose your mood, and seek out things which support and reinforce it.

It's still chilly, but the simple fact that it's dry is more than enough to lift my spirits back to the normal feelings of excitement and adventure. So come on then, let's go.

It's detour time again and I first ride south to the very spick and span looking town of Canyon, where I suspect the more affluent folk of Amarillo prefer to reside, before turning east in search of Palo Duro Canyon. As if to emphasise still further my change of mood, while I'm navigating my way through Canyon I notice a few signposts for a town called Happy. What a great address that would be to have! Back in the 19th century a group of cowboys named a nearby stream Happy Draw, for the simple reason that they were quite happy to have found it, and so the town of Happy was born. It's chosen slogan is 'the town without a frown', and I find it very surprising that despite all this unbridled joy, only six hundred or so people have chosen to make it their home. By contrast, the town of Boring in Oregon (twinned with Dull, Scotland) boasts a population around ten times that number.

Riding across the miles of flat, featureless grasslands, which make the Netherlands look positively mountainous, it's impossible to see or even imagine where on earth an 800 foot deep canyon is going to turn up. And then suddenly there it is, right before me, a delightfully lovely scenic idyll sunk deep below the surrounding plains, beautifully sheltered from the wind as well as the monotony of the wide open terrain.

Although a mere fraction of the depth of the Grand Canyon, less than half as long and a third of the width, it still ranks as the second largest canyon in America. It's not worth making comparisons though. The Grand Canyon assaults the senses like being hit by a freight train at full speed, whereas Palo Duro is gentle, calm, and feels like a sheltered and comfortable place to be.

From the edge of the plain, the access road winds its way down to the canyon floor and then continues in a loop for just a mile or so, passing a variety of camp grounds, trail heads, a riding stables, and a small outdoor theatre. There's more than enough space to lose all this lot in the landscape though, so it doesn't feel at all commercial or touristy. I follow the road for its full circuit and then park up to have a wander, and a sit, and just soak up the peace for a while. Not surprisingly, it's a lot warmer down in this sheltered haven than it is up on the open plains above; and that certainly helps in the relaxation stakes too.

The most dominant geological feature is undoubtedly Lighthouse Rock. It genuinely does look exactly like a sturdy lighthouse built on the end of a stone pier jutting out from the canyon wall, the deep sandy red of the rock giving it even more prominence as it stands silent guard over the landscape below. There's a trail running right up to the rock, but to be honest I think it looks better from a distance than it would if I were standing at its base and looking up. Obviously that's my roundabout way of saying I can't be arsed.

Palo Duro Canyon is not awe inspiring, nor sensational or breathtaking in the way that so many other landmarks manage to be. It's just a uniquely special place, peaceful and with a very serene feel about it, and definitely worthy of some time.

I sit, I wander, I admire, and I daydream. It really is a delightful spot, and it's no surprise to learn that the

Apache, Comanche and Kiowa tribes have all made it their homes at various stages of its history.

The place has already woven its magic on me when I drop into the visitor centre for a quick look around. My eye is caught by an 'educational' video playing in a perpetual loop on a screen, rather like an ad for a sensational new kind of floor mop in a supermarket. The film recounts the tale of how a number of warring Indian tribes were finally defeated at the Battle of Palo Duro Canyon in 1874. The narrator tells stories of various instances of Indian brutality towards the newly arrived white settlers, including women and children, by what he refers to as 'these vicious savages'. He goes on to argue that it's a perfectly commonplace event, repeated throughout history, for one race to displace another from its ancestral lands, and so the native Indians' cruel and murderous response to being driven from their home was of course entirely unjustified and fully deserving of the virtual annihilation which was then inflicted upon them by twenty two companies of cavalry and six of infantry.

I'm open mouthed in dismay. Yes, it might be a common occurrence, but that doesn't make it right, does it? Is it really being suggested that this slaughter was an appropriate response to a people who were, somewhat understandably, a little upset about losing the only lands and way of life that they, and countless generations before them, had ever known? I sit on a rock outside for a little while, shaking my head and wondering about what the human race really hopes to gain from its seemingly irresistible urge to justify the most appalling acts as somehow being in the interests of progress.

Back on Route 66 via the Amarillo ring road, a succession of quiet and pleasant little towns precede another collection of quirky and bizarre roadside attractions.

First, on the edge of Conway, comes the cheeky little Bug Ranch; an impudent tribute to Cadillac Ranch in the form of five VW Beetles, similarly vandalised and graffiti covered, planted into the grass on the roadside verge. Next comes the town of Groom, proudly sporting The Cross Of Our Lord Jesus Christ which claims (wrongly) to be the largest cross in the western hemisphere. It's an absolutely gigantic structure all the same, standing 190 feet tall, bright white and visible from 20 miles away on a good day. The stated purpose of the ministry based here is 'to unite all people from every continent, neighbourhood, background, race, age, and religion', although obviously with the notable exception of those Indians back up the road at Palo Duro Canyon I presume.

One such whacko gimmick isn't quite enough for this little place though. Just as I'm leaving town I have to pull over and have a smile and a chuckle at the magnificently bonkers Leaning Tower of Texas. Just a perfectly ordinary water tower, like thousands of others, but made completely unique simply by tilting it over at a wild angle. Talk about eye catching!

Next along the road comes Alanreed, a real 'blink and you missed it' little town. But don't blink, because it's very pretty with lots of trees and well-kept houses, and a fabulous old Phillips 66 petrol station – sadly now closed and gradually succumbing to the advancing undergrowth.

Late afternoon finds me rolling into McLean, a terrific looking old Route 66 town where the road actually splits to provide two parallel main streets just a block apart. In rough terms, this equates to one main street per vehicle on the road. It's a sleepy little town, established a hundred or so years ago by an Englishman who was later to perish aboard the Titanic. There's only one motel, the Cactus Inn, but that's absolutely fine because a quick show round by the proprietor reveals that it's the best motel I've found on the trip so far, and by a very good margin. Just 38 dollars for a great big room, tastefully decorated and spotlessly clean. There's a fantastic sit down shower and even a huge leather reclining chair with a built-in electric back massager, just like the ones you sometimes find at airports. Oh yes, this is a grand result. Outside it's immaculate too; the buildings are pristine and the courtyard and gardens beautifully kept, and the entrance is flanked by two giant cactus plants adorned with an array of old leather boots and a pair of cowboys legs sticking out from beneath. As you do.

I immediately book for two nights. I make a very half-hearted attempt to haggle down the already cheap rate, more through habit than serious intent, and the proprietor just smiles and gradually begins to draw the room key back across the counter. I return his smile and sign the registration form. Good that we understand each other then.

One small note though – McLean is in a 'dry' county, so be sure to bring your own booze if you want some. I hop back on the bike before I get too comfortable, and nip back down the road to cross into the next county where I can stock up with a few cans of beer.

Right next door to the Cactus Inn, the Red River Steakhouse is more than big enough to accommodate the whole town, plus most of their friends and relations too. Good wholesome food is served by good wholesome waitresses, one of whom sports the most remarkably pear-shaped figure I've ever seen. She really is shaped exactly like a pear, there's no other way to describe her. She's a lovely young lady; always smiling, very chatty, helpful and attentive – although it isn't too difficult given the number of customers she's having to serve this evening.

Dinner, for me and the two other people in the entire place, is accompanied in fine style by Buddy, a great big rotund bloke with a terrific voice, singing along to a country music karaoke tape from far away down at the other end of the empty expanse of the dining hall. He's made up for his apparent inability to play a guitar by going the whole nine yards on his authentic outfit; sporting the obligatory faded denim jeans held up by a wide leather belt with a huge buckle decorated with embossed steer horns, a black and red checked shirt with those shiny metal bits on the points of the collar, and an extremely fine looking pair of elaborately embroidered cowboy boots. The inevitable Stetson hat and a truly excellent moustache complete the look. There's a plastic bucket marked 'Bucks for Buddy' perched on the corner of the small stage and I duly oblige, as the evening would otherwise have been a deathly quiet experience.

I haven't checked until now, but it turns out there's no phone signal here, so it looks like it's going to be a rather solitary retreat; especially as I appear to be the only guest at the Cactus Inn.

5th May. 0 miles.

The Barbed Wire
Museum.

T he day breaks with a dense, clinging mist leaving absolutely zero visibility; so I'm very pleased with the previous evening's decision to take a day off the bike here. As I walk along the road towards the centre of town the air is so moist that I'm actually getting quite damp, and I'm pleased to find a welcoming looking diner after only a couple of blocks.

The Wagon Wheel Café provides as fine a fried breakfast as I've ever tasted, served by another friendly and chatty lady who, it transpires to my astonishment, is the mother of last night's pear-shaped waitress. Clearly a long lineage of waitressing in this family, but then it's that kind of town. We get chatting. She doesn't possess a passport, and has lived all her life in this tiny place with its population of about 750 people. Asking about my trip, she completely floors me with the question 'so where does Route 66 go to?' What? Seriously? You've lived beside this road all your life and you don't know where it goes? I don't say this out loud of course. There's even a little Route 66 museum just twenty yards away from the café, which would surely provide the answer if she cared to pay it a visit. Anyway, I duly inform her she has a choice of either Chicago or Los Angeles, depending on whether she turns left or right out of the door. I watch her expression as I give her this information, and she does genuinely appear to find it something of a revelation. Sipping my coffee, I find the whole thing even more peculiar when it occurs to me that she must serve and chat with several passing travellers like me every single day of every week. Surely the question of where the road leads to has cropped up a few times before?

By the end of a long leisurely breakfast, the mist has burned away and bright warm sunshine is making me feel properly on holiday again. In McLean, life happens at about a quarter of the pace of the rest of the world, and I'm loving the feeling as it slows me down too.

Just around the corner from the café I find the marvellous Devil's Rope Museum, with the self-explanatory slogan 'A Tribute To Barbed Wire'. Well I have to confess that I've never come across a museum entirely dedicated to barbed wire before, so this has to be worth a visit. It doesn't disappoint! Extensive, informative, and fascinating. Who would have imagined that such an ordinary item had such an interesting history associated with it, or came in so many varieties and shapes?

The point, if you'll pardon the pun, is that there are a lot of people in America, who between them consume an awful lot of beef, and this northern part of Texas is a place very well suited to growing beef; so much so that it's home to twice as many cattle as any other state, almost twelve million of them in total. And if you're in the business of growing beef, it's a damned nuisance if your crop keeps wandering off and disappearing over the horizon, never to be seen again. Hence – barbed wire. The truth is, when you think about it, there's probably nothing which has contributed more to the successful and economical production of beef than barbed wire – with the possible exception of grass, but I don't think a Museum of Grass would work quite so well. Apparently some 450 patents exist for varying designs of barbed wire, and in all more than 2,000 different types of wire have been identified by collectors over the years, most of which seem to be on display right here (the wire, not the collectors). So there you go, people do actually collect rusty old bits of barbed wire, and of course they even have a club called the Antique Barbed Wire Society – annual subscription 25 dollars.

In one corner there's that great little Route 66 museum I mentioned earlier too, and the town also boasts a local history museum and a nicely preserved original Phillips 66 Gas and Service Station, resplendent in gleaming orange and black paint and with a matching orange and black vintage pickup truck on the forecourt for added authenticity.

Exploring the town, which admittedly doesn't take a huge amount of time, it strikes me as a good wholesome place populated by decent and hard-working folk. Sure, it's a bit scruffy in places, but it's a busy and industrious kind of scruffy rather than abandoned and derelict. I particularly like the street names too – they've gone for a very functional and logical approach, with the main street being called First Street, the next one across named Second Street, then Third Street, all the way to Eighth Street. You only get tarmac as far as Sixth Street though – beyond that it's gravel, or mud, depending on the weather.

I really like McLean. It's another definitive example of small-town America and it's made a perfect place to spend a relaxing and enjoyable day.

With the very welcome return of the sun, I devote the late afternoon to giving the bike a thorough clean as it's looking pretty rough again after all the filth that the last few days of rain and snow have thrown all over it. The motel owner strolls across at one point, probably to check I'm not using his best towels as cleaning cloths, and we chat for a while about the weather and my trip. He gets a fair few other bikers coming through apparently, although they're normally organised groups being herded along in an orderly fashion, so I think I strike him as being rather more adventurous than most.

Flicking on the TV to check the weather before I take a shower, my attention is caught by the news that it's election day back at home. Incredibly, this is the very first time the UK election has been mentioned. There hasn't been a second of coverage until today, whereas we Brits are always made to suffer the build up to US elections in the most minute and excruciating detail for month after endless month. By comparison, the trial and court appearances of Michael Jackson on charges of child molestation are consistently accounting for around six hours of coverage per channel per day.

I round off the day sitting on the veranda outside my room, feet up and with a can of cold beer in my hand, just daydreaming and watching the warm sun slowly drift down towards the horizon. I suppose I ought to be chewing and spitting tobacco. It's good to be alive, and it's good to be in McLean.

6th May. 122 miles.

Finding My Place.

I t's invigorating to be back on the road again, now astride a clean shiny bike, and it feels great to have the sun on my face.

Leaving McLean I ride first to Shamrock, for a coffee stop and to admire the fabulous U-Drop-Inn café and Conoco gas station. It's a stunningly perfect art deco building of immense proportions, exquisitely restored to original condition and immaculate in every detail; far better than any museum because it's still alive, and the kind of place you can just stand and gaze at for ages – so I do. Testament to its grand opinion of its own status, I note that instead of having a humble car wash, this place describes its facility for the cleansing of vehicles as an 'auto laundry'.

The townsfolk of Shamrock, just like most of the population of America, make a great deal of their extremely tenuous Irish roots. I don't really understand why this is, but it does seem to be the case that having Irish ancestry is somehow a badge of honour here, with the result that just about every single person you meet seems able to lay claim to an Irish great-great-grand-something-or-other. They must have been prolific breeders, those old Irish folk.

On across the state line into Oklahoma and through the virtual ghost town of Texola, population 36. I stop at the general store, not to buy anything because it's long since closed down, but to admire and take a picture of the slogan which has been carefully painted onto the facia – *'There's no other place like this place anywhere near this place, so this must be the place'*. I really like things like this. Philosophy for the everyday man?

In the pretty little town of Sayre, the county courthouse was used as a location in John Ford's film of The Grapes of Wrath. This, to me, gives Sayre elevated status among the landmarks of my journey, as reading the Grapes of Wrath was fundamental in building my appreciation of the historical significance of this route and how it, quite literally, shaped a great deal of our modern history and culture.

Elk City is on the small side to qualify as a city in my view, boasting as it does a population of a mere 12,000 people, and notable for nothing in particular. Its cluster of museums documenting the town's development, ranch and farm life, and the 'official' National Route 66 Museum are all, frankly, disappointing. They present an unrealistically sanitised representation of what life almost certainly wasn't once like. As you'll have gathered, Route 66 museums appear in great abundance along the journey, but I'm afraid that once you've seen two or three at most, you've pretty much covered it all. There are, after all, only so many varieties of vintage petrol pump or rusty signposts.

In truth, I find the ordinary, working, unpreserved features of much more interest; like the wonderful railway goods yard and loading tower which I pass on the edge of town, all rusting corrugated iron, and somehow with a distinctly industrial beauty about it.

And so to Clinton and the Trade Winds Motel. On enquiring if I can have a peep, I'm dutifully escorted to view Room 215 where Elvis once stayed the night. It's just like all the other rooms, but perhaps ever so slightly larger and with pictures of Elvis all over the walls. I'm also treated to a private inspection of the en-suite bathroom and the toilet where Elvis... well, whatever.

Directly opposite the motel there's inevitably yet another Route 66 museum, where I have the pleasure of a good long chat with a couple from Miami who are riding an enormous bright yellow Honda Goldwing complete with trailer, stereo, satnav, and all the trimmings. I can't help wondering if they might as well have got themselves a car.

The greatest highlight of the day, though, has undoubtedly been the road itself and the passing countryside. It's old road all the way, most of it very ageing concrete rather than tarmac, laid in sections with a join every ten yards or so which produces an almost hypnotic rhythm as the tyres rumble along beating out a constant da-dum da-dum. Often, even older sections of road appear and run alongside, overgrown with lines of weeds marking the concrete joints and wonderfully evocative of the bygone days of jalopies struggling west to a desperately hoped-for new life, or sleek leather-trimmed convertibles cruising to the surf.

Meanwhile, the landscape around me has transformed itself almost completely in the space of only a few short miles. Starting with the familiar flat grasslands of Texas, first a gentle rolling begins with shallow dips as the road crosses streams by way of ageing concrete bridges; then quite quickly there are many more trees and I feel like I'm in rural England, perhaps Oxfordshire or Warwickshire, surrounded by bushy hedges and mature oak trees. It feels familiar, feels good inside. The one big difference, though, is the colour of the soil; a strikingly distinctive deep rusty red. It reminds me again of The Grapes of Wrath, or more precisely of the picture on the book's cover. Indeed, it's exactly this area which was the epicentre of the great dust bowl all those years ago, where the Joad family were finally forced to abandon their drought-stricken farm and join the countless thousands heading west to escape starvation as their soil literally turned to dust and blew away on the wind.

Another little reminder that it definitely isn't really England is the most incongruous and unfortunate sight of two armadillos lying squashed in the road. I'm too late to help them, but good karma is restored very shortly afterwards as the opportunity presents itself to rescue a surprisingly lively tortoise who's about to make a very unwise decision to try and jaywalk his way across two lanes of tarmac.

I'm finding I feel better moving than staying put on the whole. My mind and body have acquired the rhythm of constant movement and it feels uncomfortable, sort of out of place, to remain still for long. Of course I stop and see all the sights along the way, but fundamentally this is a road trip, not a sitting around and resting trip, and so continual motion is a must and I shall keep on moving, neither rushing nor dawdling, just moving at whatever pace feels right in the moment, pressing on towards Chicago and who knows quite where after that. It feels exciting, still.

Whiling away the evening with some very decent food and a few cold beers, I'm in a happy, content, and thoughtful frame of mind. I reflect on many aspects of my life, where I've been and what I've done, and where I find myself now; finding a great deal of pleasure just in the moment, and not feeling at all tempted to worry about what comes next, the future and what it may hold, what I should be doing, things I should be striving toward.

Perhaps inevitably, those wise words on the front of the general store in Texola come back to mind. *There's no other place like this place anywhere near this place, so this must be the place.* At the time I saw it, it was just another one of the multitude of quirky, mildly amusing little curiosities along the road; it made me smile and it was worthy of a short break in my journey and a quick photograph. But the more I think about it, the more I realise just how much significance it holds for me, how strongly it resonates with me. The message is suddenly so clear.

I know I've been learning something about myself as this trip unfolds, and that simple slogan daubed across the wall of a building has brought some clarity to exactly what it is. It's all so obvious. It makes sense. Wherever I am at any given moment, just accept that it's the right place to be. No real need to fully understand why it's the right place, or why or how I came to be there, just soak it in and make the most of it. Experience the place, look around and really see it, smell it, feel it, hear the sounds and enjoy it; learn anything there might be to learn from it, and then move on to the next place. And when you get there, that will also be the right place, for its own little period of time. Sure, keep an occasional eye on the map just to check that each of these places is taking you roughly in the direction of your ultimate goal. But don't get so completely hung up on the goal that you forget to immerse yourself in all the other 'right' places you travel through along the way.

I know we're all supposed to have goals in life, ambitions towards which we must strive; and I'm not saying that's a bad thing by any means. But I see so many people who are always so completely focussed on where they want to get to that they never notice or appreciate where they actually are at the present moment, never allow themselves time to take off the blinkers and look around and enjoy their surroundings, always working towards a goal or a destination and forgetting to take pleasure in the here and now, in all the different places and experiences that make up the journey.

I didn't know it at the time, but the growing popularity of this way of thinking would soon take it past the tipping point into mainstream awareness and give it a name – Mindfulness.

To this day I've never read a book on mindfulness; and I rather suspect that I never will. Nor do I ever sit cross legged with my eyes closed and my palms turned upwards, because I just don't do that kind of stuff. Except clearly I do. I just do it in my own way, and my way is travel. Travelling through different places, and recognising in every single case that 'this must be the place.' And of course it's not always some Zen-like place filled with peace, flowers and beautiful birdsong. In its own special way, the place can just as easily be a rain-lashed motorway in a howling crosswind with a 40-ton truck bearing down on you. It might not do much for your inner calm, but it'll certainly add to the rich tapestry of experiences that make up who you are.

I realise that it's for this reason, too, that I tend not to like rigid itineraries. A long journey with every day's route and every overnight stop mapped out in advance means you've effectively determined which are the 'places' you're going to experience before you've even seen them. And inevitably those aren't going to be the special places that just appear by chance or fortune along the way. You'll miss out on those. Why? Because you've made yourself a slave to the ultimate goal.

I won't deny it though, there's still a lot to be said for proper planning and goal setting in all aspects of life. If you are one of life's planners then hats off to you, but let me recommend you try something, even if it's only once. Just try not having a plan, going with the flow, living in the moment – because you might enjoy it.

There's a flip side to this 'being in the right place' thinking too, of course, because there are plenty of times when we find ourselves in the *wrong* place. If you don't like the place you're in right now, be it a physical place on a map or the place that your head's in, then it's time to move on, go somewhere else, somewhere better. The more I think about it, the more obvious and simple I realise it is. You hear people all the time saying things like 'Oh I just hate living in London'. Fine, well you should move somewhere else then. It'll make you happier. You can spend every day standing on a street corner with a megaphone shout-ing about how much you dislike London, but you'll still be in London. That won't change until *you* change it. It's the same for the 'My life's so awful, I've got the weight of the world on my shoulders' brigade. The constant victims, who tell you endlessly about how they could have achieved so much if only it wasn't for this, that, or the other. Sure, you've got some problems and not everything is perfect, but it's the same for all of us from time to time. It doesn't matter how much you moan about it, you'll stay in exactly the same place until you do something about it yourself, until you change some things, and move on to a better place.

This Must Be The Place.

7th May. 221 miles.

Mother Of The Mother Road.

The architecture and the road construction techniques tell me I'm in America today, whilst the landscape continues to insist that I'm really in England and the overcast but very pleasantly warm weather ensures that wherever I am, I'm enjoying every moment.

Gently rolling lush green countryside with fertile farmland fills me with the joys of spring, whilst delightfully picturesque farmhouses and outbuildings keep the camera shutter clicking.

I'm heading for Oklahoma City first, along wonderful old roadbed made of concrete with moulded kerbs, as solid and sound today as it was sixty or more years ago when it was built. I'm often tracked on one side or the other by even older sections, straight and narrow and laid like a long brown ribbon across the undulating landscape, while the soulless interstate forces its unnatural course through cuttings and over embankments, succeeding in being the means to its end, but failing to appreciate the myriad sights and experiences which really define the journey.

I've mentioned already my admiration for steel truss bridges, and today they're in plentiful supply. Clean, simple, probably quite heavily over-engineered, and obviously built in an age when a job was worth doing properly. I think when I grow old I'm going to need to acquire an anorak and a beard and join an appreciation society for these things.

Near Hydro, Lucille's Gas Station is one of the great landmarks of Route 66. It's a distinctive design; a very small building with just the office and a pair of petrol pumps at ground level, and the owners accommodation on the first floor extending over the forecourt and pumps to form a protective canopy. Lucille Hamons bought the place in 1941 and operated it non-stop and singlehandedly for the rest of her life. The help she gave to motorists during the tough times at the end of the great depression earned her the nickname 'The Mother of the Mother Road', and the boom times of the 50's and 60's helped the business thrive. The completion of the Interstate in 1971 brought an abrupt end to the majority of Lucille's trade, but she still carried on undaunted for another 29 years until her death on 18th August 2000. A little bizarrely, the place was then sold on Ebay; but the good news is that it's ended up being restored and preserved as it deserves to be.

The town of El Reno is in party mode, with a huge

custom car show in progress and a carnival atmosphere along the main street. I stroll amongst rows of fantastic hot rods – Model T's, Corvettes, Chevys, all outrageously pimped and with their vast chromed and supercharged V8's glistening in the sunshine.

A navigational cock up on the way through Oklahoma City keeps me on my toes and continually pulling over to try and fathom out where the hell I am, until I find a reliable landmark in the form of the famous Round Barn at Arcadia, and pull into the car park of the Hillbillies Bed and Breakfast Inn next door.

There's clearly something big going on as the car park is packed with a hundred or so bikers, all pretty hard core looking Harley dudes. Most people would steer well clear but I know better, and I'm proved right as a cold bottle of beer is thrust into my hand before I've even swung my leg off the bike; and two hours of banter and interest and envy over my trip duly ensues.

The bikers are apparently engaged in something called a 'Poker Run', which I deduce after much bafflement consists of a sort of treasure hunt where you stop at checkpoints, drink beer, and get handed a playing card at random which ends up having something to do with a poker hand. I've never since bothered to look up the real details, as the crowd taking part seemed similarly unconcerned with the finer points of the game; it was about the camaraderie and a good day out, and that's all that really matters.

I only just remember to have a look at the barn too,

before moving on. It's a hundred years old, red, round, and made of wood, including the perfectly domed roof.

A succession of one horse, and one street, towns eventually brings me into Sapulpa where I decide it's about time to call it a day and hunt out a bed. A very friendly bunch of folk around the bar later make for a great evening, and it's most refreshing to chat with two of them in particular - a travelling salesman and the barmaid - who have both actually travelled to a good extent and display a keen interest in geography and culture which extends well beyond that of most of those I've met thus far.

Oddly, I can't sleep very well. I keep finding myself lying awake and worrying about money, which is completely unnecessary as I've left everything well organised and in good order. I think it's more just the general principle that you shouldn't go away on a jaunt for six weeks when everyone else is busy earning a living, and that's what's nagging at me. I need to snap out of it and realise that all those people busy slaving away on the treadmill would probably give their right arm for the chance of a trip like this. I also need to remember that the last thing I did before leaving was to send out a good batch of invoices, and there'll be more ready to go as soon as I'm home again. The mortgage is covered, as are all the other bills, so stop wasting energy worrying and get on with the adventure. What really matters is the feeling of freedom and the powerful sense that I can do anything I want to. Not many people can say that.

I manage to pull myself round, and finally suc-
cumb to sleep smiling in amusement at the wildlife I
saw today. Yesterday it was squashed armadillos and
a tortoise, and today I was entertained by the rather
comical sight of a roadrunner, which true to form
was running along the road. They're hilarious looking
creatures, like a chicken on steroids.

8th May. 232 miles.

A Bit Of A Moment.

I have to confess to waking with more than a slight headache for the first time on the trip. Damn those sociable Americans last night! So what, it was a cracking evening, and I'm still up and out before 10.00 am.

A bout of inspired route finding leads me neatly through the centre of Tulsa, which is a fairly well to do town with leafy suburbs and lots of those fine old wooden houses with verandas which you see in the films depicting the orderly and sanitised (I just typed that as 'satanised', ironically) version of American living.

A rain shower has evidently preceded me through town by only a few minutes, and on the outskirts I have my first real 'moment', as we motorcyclists like to refer to close-run flirtations with disaster and significant personal injury and inconvenience.

It's a textbook hazard situation which I should have seen coming a mile off. Traffic lights change, catching me unprepared; which is stupid, because what the hell else do traffic lights ever do apart from change? I hit the brakes a bit smartish. It's a two lane road, where the cars sit dripping a little oil in the outside lane while they wait at red, and trucks sit dripping loads of oil in the inside lane. I'm in the inside lane. Lovely and oily, with rain on top; oh yes, it's slippery alright. To make matters worse, it's right in front of a café where a dozen or so bikers are gathered outside and treated to a grandstand view as my rear wheel makes a spirited attempt to overtake the front wheel, leaving me with a slightly raised pulse rate and a tightly clenched sphincter.

There are a number of well known laws surrounding biking mishaps, with this one about always having a good sized audience when you mess things up being high on the list. It's also a proven fact that you will only ever have a puncture if you're travelling without a puncture repair kit, and that you will realise you haven't done up your helmet buckle only after you've put your gloves on. I could go on.

The lights change and I pull away extremely gently, yet still the wheel struggles for any grip until I'm half way across the junction. The rain soon brings me to a stop once again, under full control this time, to shelter beneath a tree for a little while.

The Blue Whale is Tulsa's contribution to the bizarre roadside attraction hall of fame. This giant concrete representation of something looking vaguely like a whale with a big smile and googly eyes, a water slide sticking out of the side of its head, and sporting a baseball cap, sits rather forlornly in what was once a small waterpark but is now just an overgrown pond filled with green slime. I imagine it's a good few years since it heard the sound of children's laughter.

The next stretch of 66 is a proper road in full use, and even dual carriageway for much of the time. After Oklahoma City, Interstate 40 carries on more or less due west through Tennessee and North Carolina whereas Route 66 turns to head in a north easterly direction and is now broadly tracked by the Will Rogers Turnpike, aka Highway 44, with the two roads being of more or less equal prominence.

The Totem Pole Park at Foyil provides an interesting diversion; one man's life's work creating an extensive and varied collection of huge totem poles, now all nicely restored and freshly painted.

One of the guidebooks has told of some rare stretches of original single-track roadway between Afton and Miami (not *that* Miami), constructed only eight feet wide as the state was a little strapped for cash at the time, what with it being the Great Depression and all that. I search for ages in vain until I finally give up the hunt and ride on towards Miami – and promptly find exactly what I've been looking for. It's not driveable for any great distance, but I'm amazed at just how deeply a bit of cracked tarmac can stir the senses.

I now cross into Kansas, but not for long. Kansas is only able to boast a mere fourteen miles of Route 66, but they've milked it for all it's worth by painting the 66 shield logo onto the tarmac about every 200 yards. And judging by the quality of some of the artwork involved, I think they may have entrusted the local schoolchildren with the project.

Beyond Joplin, many lovely stretches of original road come and go like quiet country backroads, and the enormous screen of a drive-in cinema rears high into the sky approaching Carthage. It's still in use as well, and they're showing Miss Congeniality 2. I'd love to go just for the experience but I think it would get a little uncomfortable sitting astride a bike all evening, and probably a bit chilly too.

I decide to spend the night in Carthage, and am warmly greeted by a wonderfully jolly hotel receptionist who very kindly offers to take care of all my laundry for me. Do I really smell that bad, I wonder? I snap her hand off in any case. It's a real luxury to have absolutely everything clean and fresh, and even better that it doesn't require any hassle or waiting around on my part.

I don't really know why I was feeling rather low yesterday. Just one of those days I think, for the world all seems fine again today and, thinking about it, I've been smiling more or less continually all day. I must have subconsciously decided to move on to a better place. It's been a bit of a day for receiving compliments today actually, so maybe that's helped as well. I've been informed on two occasions that I have a lovely accent, and both times by beautiful ladies too, one of whom was even sufficiently moved to keep me in her company for a while longer by giving me a free cup of coffee as I paid her for my petrol! There was definitely a hot dinner date in the offing there if I'd been so inclined. A friendly gentleman also said I had a very nice jacket, although he stopped short of treating me to a free drink.

The nature of the road has changed fundamentally now. It seems more run of the mill and every day. It's still beautiful in places, but the awe inspiring scenery and the sense of pioneering adventure have faded, as have the characters who contribute as much as the terrain and the road itself to making Route 66 what it is. Don't get me wrong, the people are lovely and very friendly, but they're just not 'characters' in quite the same way.

9th May. 231 miles.

The Bar Full Of Bras.

I kick off the day with an early morning stroll around the pretty town square, dominated by its ridiculously grand, almost cathedral-like town hall. Then I'm back onto the bike heading east on a fairly busy road for a little while, when much older and bypassed sections appear and tempt me into a charmingly slow and relaxed journey along many forgotten miles of old highway which roll and swoop around long lazy curves, tracing the contours of the landscape through verdant valleys alongside glistening streams and peaceful little communities nestling just yards from the new road, yet completely calm and hidden from view.

Through Springfield I take a short detour to visit what claims to be 'The Worlds Biggest Outdoor Store'. It certainly is massive, and I'm particularly taken with the legend which hangs above the front door. 'Welcome Fishermen, Hunters, and other Liars'.

Onwards through Strafford, Conway, and Lebanon

and a photo stop at the brilliant neon sign which announces the famous Munger Moss Motel. Continuing past Waynesville, the scenery in this area known as the Ozark Plateau is truly fantastic. Countless miles of completely unspoiled mature forests, interspersed with lush green pastures and charming old wooden farms and chalets complete with their immaculate picket fences, some with rusting old vintage pickup trucks parked out front with the grass growing around and even through them, and an optimistic price tag daubed in whitewash paint across the windscreen.

And of course there's always the amazing old road, cracked and largely deserted but still somehow very much alive, weaving its way through the countryside completely at ease with every contour of the land.

It's around here that I encounter my first 'Meramec Barn'. More on the Meramec Caverns themselves later, when I get there, but for now a little about these barns. It's fair to say that Lester Dill, who bought the Meramec Caverns to develop as a tourist attraction in 1933, was a man who liked customers. He really liked them a great deal, and especially in large numbers; and in order to bring them flocking to his caverns, he went to enormous lengths of both effort and ingenuity to ensure the message got out there – so much so in fact, that it's impossible to miss it even to this day. Lester would regularly jump into his car and drive great distances in both directions along Route 66, looking out for prominent barns in fields by the roadside. Each time he happened upon such a building, he would drive into the yard and enquire of the farmer whether he would like his barn to receive a fresh coat of paint – for free.

'And what's the catch?' would come the inevitable reply from a farmer tempted by a free offer, but at the same time a little suspicious. The deal was simply that Lester would gladly paint the entire barn, so long as he could do it in garishly bright colours and daub messages such as 'Meramec Caverns 70 miles ahead' in letters ten feet high along the side of the barn which faced the road. It's clear that the farmers of America very much like a bargain, and aren't overly concerned with the aesthetic beauty of their outbuildings, because before long the countryside was littered with brightly coloured Meramec Barns, many of which are now preserved as national historic monuments. It's also claimed that, in addition to painting many a dull barn in outrageous colour schemes, Mr Dill also invented the bumper sticker as another means of widespread promotion of his burgeoning tourism enterprise.

As well as being both creative and industrious, it seems that Lester Dill was also blessed with a considerable degree of good fortune. What's that saying about 'the harder I work, the luckier I get'? Having initially bought a fairly modestly sized cavern, he subsequently made a number of discoveries of new passageways and hidden chambers which left him with a significantly larger hole in the ground than he'd paid for.

Back to the road, and it's pretty obvious that I'm travelling through the Bible Belt region now. Churches by the hundred all around, and endless signs urging me to see the light and join the throng. Both time and inclination are against that, and so is serendipity it seems, as by chance I happen across the Devil's Elbow Inn, tucked away a few yards down a side road in an enchanting little hidden river valley just next to another lovely old bridge.

It's clearly a biker's boozing den, although only a couple of folk are here today. I park up next to their bikes and enter the rustic old wooden shack of a bar for a leisurely beer and a friendly chat with an archetypal long-beard-and-leather-waistcoat biker type. He's a great character, the kind of bloke who would comfortably stand his ground against an oncoming freight train, such is the size of his frame, and with shovel-like hands which dwarf a bottle of Miller Lite so much that it looks more like a miniature. Despite his imposing stature, he has gentle kind eyes which look like they've seen a fair few experiences and come out stronger and wiser and generally at peace with the world. And there was me thinking only yesterday that the supply of colourful personalities had begun to dry up!

Strangely, it's a good five minutes or so before I become accustomed to the dim lighting and the bizarre collection of ceiling decorations catches my eye.

Every inch of it is covered in a multi-coloured sea of bras. Frilly, lacy, leather, studded, tiny, enormous, every imaginable size and type; most signed by their donors from all corners of the country and indeed the world. How very creative and highly unusual. I'm also amused by the way they promote their souvenir t-shirts – with a big sign saying 'buy a shirt you cheap bastard or I'll start dating your daughter.' Yep, it's a typical bloke's biker bar alright.

On and on I ride through yet more absolutely lovely countryside, continually taking my breath away with its simple yet stunning beauty. It's really very difficult finding the right words to describe it. Mile upon mile of gently rolling hills and river valleys, heavily forested by ancient deciduous woodlands with occasional open areas of well-tended fields around small rustic farmsteads.

The town of Rolla adds thirty minutes to the day with some navigational confusion, in fact I'm convinced that Lonely Planet have finally made a mistake, but I eventually arrive safe at the Wagon Wheel Motel in Cuba where I'm greeted, after hunting around for signs of life for ten minutes, by the friendly and jovial proprietor who introduces himself as Harold Armstrong and proudly informs me that he still runs this place entirely single-handedly despite his 78 years. It's certainly old, run down and a little smelly (the motel, not Harold), but for 16 dollars a night I can hardly complain can I? Actually, upon collecting my key and entering my room, perhaps I can. The bedspread is very grubby indeed and filled with holes, some of them caused by cigarettes and others by vermin I suspect, and in the shower there's a bloody great big cockroach. What the hell, I should have known I wasn't going to get much for 16 dollars, and it's all part of the adventure – not that I yet know quite how much a part of the adventure this place is about to play.

It's still only late afternoon, so I take the opportunity to give the bike a good scrub before braving the wildlife in the shower and then heading out in the early evening to fill my belly. I don't have to walk more than a few yards before being unable to resist the temptation of the Missouri Hick BBQ and Steakhouse, with its decidedly hillbilly appearance and an enticing meaty aroma wafting into the street.

Finishing a good wholesome dinner, I lean back in my chair feeling thoroughly beefed-out, stretch my legs out under the table, and sigh that contented sigh which says so much about what a fulfilling day it's been. I'm dog tired, but so very satisfied, happy and content.

A 'Meramec Barn'.

10th May. 45 miles.

The Murderer's Boyfriend.

I can see through the tatty window blind that it's already a perfect sunny day, and as soon as I've recovered from being startled by another cockroach joining me in the shower, I'm eagerly loading up the bike in anticipation of today's instalment of adventures.

I fire up the engine, kick back the side stand, and – I can barely move the bike an inch backwards out of its parking space. It feels like I've parked in a great pool of heavy glue. I look around, puzzled. No, I'm not trying to push it backwards uphill, for that is exactly what it feels like. Has the engine seized? Have I been riding along looking at a false reading every time I've checked the oil level? No of course not, the engine's running and it's not even in gear yet, I'm still trying to push it backwards. The brakes seem perfectly free too. Then I spot the rear tyre – splayed wide and soft and flat as a pancake.

I cut the engine and quietly consider the situation. Actually, on closer inspection I can see it's not completely flat, so maybe I can pump it up and carefully ride the seventy miles on to St. Louis where I know the hire company has a depot who will surely sort it all out.

I pop round to the motel office where, to my grateful astonishment, good old Harold gives a thoughtful rub of his bristly grey chin and then instantly produces an industrial sized air compressor. We soon have the tyre fully inflated again, and then watch forlornly as it immediately hisses flat, leaving me in an equally deflated state. It was only the stiffness in the tyre's sidewall which had held the rim clear of the ground, rather than any retained air. Ok, this bike is going nowhere fast. Better move on to Plan B.

I call the hire company for assistance. They tell me they'll gladly change the tyre for me, and all I need to do is get it to their workshop in St. Louis. I suppose I'd imagined something a little more comprehensive in terms of service and support when I'd paid the extra money for breakdown cover, and certainly didn't expect to find that it's the responsibility of the customer to ensure that any breakdowns only occur on the premises of one of the firm's various franchises. But the situation is what it is, and in simple terms that means I'm screwed.

When the going gets screwed, the screwed need coffee. So I walk round to the Missouri Hick for refreshment. I sip my drink and ponder the situation. I'm no real stranger to tricky situations, and in no time my mind is clear as to where the solution lies. It's a perfect moment to go with the flow, and invest every ounce of my faith and trust in serendipity and the kindness of strangers. It's taken me forty or so years to learn this, and now is the time to put the theory to a proper test. So I decide stage one is to do precisely nothing and just be patient, relax and see what happens.

I order another coffee and half-heartedly ask the young waitress the rather pointless question of whether she knows anyone who could fix me up with a new motorbike tyre. Of course she does! She pops into the back room and in a moment returns with my knight in shining armour, whose name is Chris. He pulls off his chef's apron, wipes his hands, and loads me straight into his car. We drive first back to the bike to get the exact tyre specifications, and then set off down the road to the custom bike shop at the far end of town. I glance at the scrap of paper on which Chris has scribbled the tyre details. It's an attendance record card from the local parole office. Oh shit. I've placed my faith in the kindness of strangers, and my stranger is on parole.

Chris sees me looking at the card and explains that it isn't him but his girlfriend who is on parole, and indeed has been for some seven years now. By my calculations, that's got to add up to a reasonably serious crime. I decide it's probably best not to enquire further, but he tells me anyway. 'Yeah they sent her down for murder, but she swears to this day she didn't do it and I believe her.' Hmmm, a jury clearly didn't though did they, and there's no mention of any appeal.

The people at the bike shop are wonderful. They don't have the right size of tyre, but without even being asked they pick up the phone and call around until they find someone who does – a little bike repair workshop fifteen miles further along the road in Rolla, and happy to set off straight away to pick up both me and the bike. While we're sorting all this out, and getting Chris into trouble for not being at work, I notice him mooching around the shop and admiring a Harley-Davidson branded signet ring sitting in a glass display cabinet. I buy the ring for him and he looks a little embarrassed as he drives me back to the restaurant, where I park myself on a bench in the sunshine to wait for the rescue truck to arrive and ponder at the marvellous nature of people. Soon one of Chris's colleagues comes out from the kitchen to find me, and thanks me profusely for making his day with the gift of the ring. I'm very happy to have been able to do so, and in all fairness I reckon Chris has made quite a positive impact on my day too.

A little time later, a rather oily individual wearing overalls and driving a big breakdown truck pulls into the car park and strides towards the restaurant door. I approach him and ask if he's come to pick up a biker, to which he responds 'Huh?', and promptly turns bright pink and rushes inside just as I realise the rather unfortunate connotation of my choice of phrase.

The next breakdown truck to arrive is mine, and we soon have the bike loaded up and shipped back down the road to Interstate Motorcycles which turns out to be, amongst other things, a Royal Enfield dealership. I exchange stories of Enfield adventures in India with the owner as he works on removing the wheel and the tyre, before triumphantly holding up the culprit in the form of a rusty inch-long steel screw. Bill 'Slam' Dunkus is one of life's eternally cheerful and positive characters, and it's a joy to share his company for an hour or so as he fits and balances my new tyre and also gives the bike a good check over while it's up on the hydraulic platform in his immaculate workshop – the walls adorned with all manner of parts, neatly labelled, and the floor so clean I'd happily eat my dinner off it.

Bill eventually pronounces the bike 'good to go', and presents me with a free t-shirt as I fire up the engine once again and head thankfully on my way. I shall be eternally grateful for the kindness and helpfulness shown to me today by complete strangers, all extremely generous with their time, effort, and initiative in the quest to help out someone they've never seen before, and never will again. Thank you all, and I will do my bit to return the favour wherever and whenever the opportunity presents itself.

Another piece of good luck which today brings is that, thanks to the delay, I only manage to make it as far as Stanton and the Meramec Caverns before it's time to pull up for the night. I arrive just in time to catch my own private tour of the caverns, which turn out to be a very excellent and beautiful system of show caves with many impressive rock formations, and climaxing in a home grown 'son et lumiere' show involving projected images of the Stars and Stripes accompanied by the piped strains of the Star Spangled Banner – it could only happen here!

It's a somewhat amateur, yet clearly well-rehearsed performance. As I slowly make my way from each section of cave to the next, the chap escorting me in his role as chief sound and lighting technician deftly flicks switches, strategically positioned on the walls, to light up the next few yards of cavern and plunge the previous section back into darkness, and all the while glancing at his watch as the hands creep alarmingly close to knocking off time.

Emerging back into the daylight, the place is entirely deserted save for a group of Amish folk, the men with their uniform blue shirts and braces and domed hats and the ladies with headscarves and crisp white pinafores. I've never encountered Amish people before, and am intrigued yet respectful of their shyness and reluctance to interact with anyone outside of their own community.

I check into the on-site motel for the night and sit out on the terrace to write up the day's diary of events, accompanied by a cold beer and a picnic supper beside the lovely and tranquil Meramec River, listening to birdsong and watching the sun slowly set, and with this whole paradise almost completely to myself.

I feel very, very lucky indeed to be experiencing all this; and so to whoever dropped that screw back at the Wagon Wheel Motel – my thanks even go out to you too.

11th May. 299 miles.

A Bridge With A Kink.

Peering out of the window, I'm pleased to see not only that both tyres are round and firm, but also that the sky is again blue and cloudless. Time to get back at it with a vengeance and clock up some miles.

I'm away by 9.00 and it's already so warm that I need to ride with my jacket zipped half way down in order the get some air flowing around those places which can get a bit too hot and sticky for comfort. As with most other days so far in this part of the country, virtually all of the old road remains in place and ride-able, and I'm loving every moment.

Following the guidebook's advice, I detour a little way south near the town of Eureka (I suppose they were very pleased to find it?) to visit the Shrine of the Black Madonna. I'm welcomed by a large and un-equivocal 'No Motorcycles' sign which I duly ignore, and spend the grand total of ten minutes looking around a collection of grottos made by sticking odd shaped stones, sea shells, and pieces of broken glass into cement. I'm sure it's the product of a lifetime's effort and devotion, but I'm afraid I can't help departing with the simple question 'Why?' uppermost in my mind. In hindsight, it would have been a better idea to obey the rather unfriendly sign at the entrance.

Around me, the countryside is now giving way to urban sprawl as I enter Missouri's second largest city, St. Louis. My sense of direction impresses me as I find my way directly to the huge Gateway Arch which towers over the banks of the mighty Mississippi River. Mind you, you can hardly miss it. 630 feet high and clad in shiny stainless steel, the arch was first conceived in 1933 with the spectacularly vague purpose of acting as a 'monument to the western expansion of the United States'; but it took until the early 60's to get around to actually building it, so I guess a committee was involved. Nonetheless, it's sufficiently impressive to warrant a coffee stop, so I pull up next to a couple who are travelling across the country on a big BMW touring bike and we chat for a while.

It's interesting comparing our two mighty steeds – theirs is designed specifically with long distance touring in mind, while I think mine is aimed more at cruising a couple of miles down the strip on a sunny weekend afternoon and hanging out with the gang. So they've got streamlined fairings and a big windshield to protect them from the elements, cruise control and a stereo system for eating up the long motorway miles with ease and comfort, a cavernous luggage system which just clips on and off in a second, integrated satnav and electronically adjusting suspension – the list goes on. And as for me – I've got a couple of fixed pannier bags with leather straps and fiddly buckles, another bag strapped roughly across the passenger seat, and no creature comforts at all. But hey, I wonder which of us feels the greater sense of adventure and achievement?

I follow the river bank northwards, passing through very depressed and rather threatening neighbourhoods before crossing the river on Interstate 270 and peeling off again on the east bank to admire the magnificent old Chain of Rocks Bridge, built in 1929 to carry Route 66 across the Mississippi; although I don't stay very long as I'm surrounded by some pretty rough looking fishermen who seem intent on fixing me with unwelcoming stares, and also because there's an overpowering stench of rotting fish.

There's a very peculiar feature to this bridge, which must make it rank quite highly among the great engineering cock-ups of all time, in that it has a 22 degree bend right in the middle of it which continually caused large trucks to get stuck while trying to negotiate it. Folk put up with the inconvenience for 35 years before deciding enough was enough and building a new bridge, which had the considerable advantage of being straight, just a matter of yards upstream and rendering the original crossing obsolete. And so today it stands as possibly the world's most over-engineered pedestrian footbridge.

In crossing the Mississippi, I've entered the final State on Route 66 – Illinois – and it immediately becomes apparent that someone in this State knows how to do signposting properly. It's not that Missouri, and many other States too, don't have plenty of signs; merely that they're not particularly adept at putting them in the right places. Illinois, by contrast, has every junction clearly and accurately signposted which saves a great deal of time in not needing to stop and check the map every five minutes. Strangely, though, it isn't long before I'm asking myself whether this actually takes away some of the sense of adventure. There's a continual debate among touring bikers over the pros and cons of the satnav, and whether you lose something special by removing the possibility of getting lost.

Personally, I'm firmly on the side of getting lost every now and again, as this has resulted in finding myself in many wonderful places which I would have sailed right past if I'd had technology guiding me constantly in the right direction. On the other hand, I've also found myself getting thoroughly fed up after completing the fifteenth lap of some dreadful one way system which seems to have no exit. So I guess in truth I think that satnavs are a bad thing, except for when they're a good thing. And let's not even get started on the whole question of how reliable the damn things are in any case! Anyway, thanks to the good folk in the Illinois Highways Department, they're certainly not needed here.

The locals in this part of the state display an exemplary commitment to the preservation of vintage fuel stations, which I suppose is to be expected of a nation whose heritage is so inextricably entwined with the motor car. The Soulsby Service Station in Mount Olive is a lovely example of the 1920's design template of a small shop and office with an elegant canopy extending over the pumps, all immaculately decked out in the Shell colours and a far cry from the dreadful bolt-together standardised corporate rubbish we have to suffer today. Further up the road in Odell the Standard Oil Gas Station is of a near identical design from the same era, and also worthy of a brief stop for a photo.

Pulling in for fuel just south of Springfield (there's an awful lot of Springfields in America) I see there's a missed call on my phone from a UK number. Calling back, I find it's my sister on a borrowed phone, who tells me that my mum has been taken into hospital this morning with severe stomach pains. It's very concerning to receive this kind of news when you're thousands of miles away and in no position to do anything useful about it, but she assures me there's no major cause for alarm. The initial theory of appendicitis has been dropped in favour of some kind of infection, and she promises to keep me updated by text message.

I cross my fingers and carry on, through Springfield to Lincoln where something very strange happens. Within the space of no more than five minutes the weather has changed from still, sunny and with the temperature in the low 90's, to overcast, suddenly cold, and with a strong northerly headwind buffeting me so hard it feels as though my arms are going to be torn from their sockets at any moment and the helmet ripped clean off my head, possibly even with my head still inside. The remainder of the day's ride, through Bloomington and Normal to Pontiac, becomes a real physical battle which leaves me with aching shoulders and feeling more than ready for a beer and a bite to eat. I know I keep banging on about how wonderful these bikes are, but I'll admit they do have rather a weakness when it comes to high speed riding, or lower speeds with a headwind. You're sitting with your back more or less upright, and your legs outstretched to the front, and with nothing to shield your upper body from the wind that's hitting you. The result is that the full force has to be taken by your arms holding the handlebars, and it can amount to quite some force too, for hours or maybe even days on end. This is why proper touring bikes have fairings and wind shields, and why my decision to opt for a completely inappropriate type of bike just because it looks cool does come at a cost. Mind you, should I ever find myself clinging by my finger tips to the edge of a cliff, I'll happily be able to dangle there for as long as is necessary.

It's an evening of mixed feelings, as tomorrow I will reach downtown Chicago, the end of the road as far as Route 66 is concerned.

Standard Oil gas station, Odell.

12th May. 137 miles.

Farewell 66.

The day begins with wet, but rapidly drying, tarmac so I buy an extra-large coffee and take my time over packing and getting organised and set off around 10.00 am, by which time the roads are largely dry. The inch-perfect Illinois signposts remain as consistent as ever, and today I do appreciate them as they lead me through a couple of lovely little towns which I otherwise would surely have missed. Odell and Dwight are both picture perfect old places, whitewashed to the nines, and bypassed before bypasses were even invented.

I'm also neatly guided to the unmissable Gemini Giant in Wilmington. Standing the best part of thirty feet high, decked out in green overalls and a silver space helmet which actually looks remarkably like a welders face shield, and holding a silver space rocket, this fine fellow definitely ranks as one of the best, and also best-preserved, examples of Route 66 'Muffler Men'. The story of the Muffler Men begins in 1962 when Bob Prewett, who owned the Prewett Fiberglass boat building company, took on a rather unusual commission and constructed a huge statue of Paul Bunyan, a legendary giant lumberjack in US folklore, as a roadside promotion for the Paul Bunyan Café all the way back down the road in Flagstaff, Arizona.

When Steve Dashew bought the boatbuilding business a year later, the mould was still knocking around the back of the workshop, and he spotted the opportunity for a lucrative sideline to the main business of building boats. Over the next ten years, hundreds of the statues were commissioned in all sorts of different guises, but all originating from the same mould and with the same basic shape. The original statue held out an axe in front of him, but the arrangement of arms and hands held out forwards allowed for pretty much anything to be substituted, and in many cases the statues were used to advertise vehicle workshops and held exhaust pipes (or mufflers), hence the nickname.

The Gemini Giant, by the way, serves to catch the attention of potential customers for the adjacent Launching Pad Drive-In restaurant, hence the spaceman variant in the design. I bid him a good day and travel onwards, past the communities of Ellwood and Joliet, which of course lent their names to the legendary Blues Brothers in the film of the same name. I must get hold of a copy of that film, as well as Bagdad Café. Needless to say, I already have Easy Rider.

Reaching the outskirts of Chicago I detour to take a

look at 'The Spindle', a quirky work of art in the form of a huge steel spike upon which a stack of eight old cars are skewered. It turns out to be in the middle of a shopping mall car park, and not at all as impressive as I had been led to believe. The pigeons seem to quite like it though.

I ride on, passing through run down suburbs, and all the while closing in on the cluster of skyscrapers which mark downtown Chicago in the distance ahead of me. Entering the heart of the city is very much like riding into a deep, dark ravine, as the tower blocks reach straight up to the clouds and I, along with all the other people and cars and buses and trucks, seem rather like tiny children's toys on the street far below. The final half mile brings me over a slight crest from where twenty sets of traffic lights stretch before me, all changing in perfect unison. And beyond the last lights the concrete jungle abruptly ends, a small sign announces quietly yet clearly the end of Route 66, and I emerge into the open air of Grant Park with the endless expanse of Lake Michigan disappearing to the horizon.

After following this amazing road for twenty three of the most extraordinary, exhilarating, and enjoyable days of my life, I've finally reached its end. It's a road which ends properly too; it doesn't just fade out or turn into some other road, but runs smack into Lake Michigan. It's the same if you travel in the other direction too of course, as on arriving at Santa Monica you're also faced with the choice of either stopping or getting wet.

It's chilly and blustery with leaden clouds racing from the lake across the city, and the sight of cold waves splashing up over the edge of the harbour makes it pretty clear that I'm not going one inch further. It's a good way, exactly the right way, for such a special and legendary road to end.

I park up and eat a sandwich next to a large fountain in the park, trying as best I can to take in where I am and what I have done. There does seem to be a rather surreal quality to the experience, and I sit quietly entranced, pondering the fact that I've just completed an adventure which, for most people who think of it, never finds its way off the bucket list and into reality. At this moment my daydreaming is interrupted by a text message to say that all is well with mum, which is great news and couldn't be better timed.

Route 66 has become a close friend and faithful companion. It isn't just a stretch of tarmac. It's also known as the Main Street of America and as the Mother Road; and both names suit it well. It's given me a great adventure, and showed me the heart of an extraordinary and surprisingly little known or understood country. Everyone thinks they know exactly what America's like, but they honestly don't – all they know is the version of America that they see in films and on the TV, and that's not the real America, it really isn't. The road, and my own journey along it, has also changed me; leaving me more at ease with the world, and more confident in my own ability to move through life calmly, with a sense of balance, with confidence, wisdom, and perspective.

Farewell Route 66, and thank you for an incredible ride.

I could stay the night here in Chicago. I feel I ought to explore such a city as this while I'm here, find a suitable hotel and spend the rest of the afternoon and evening seeing some of the sights. But it doesn't appeal at all. I'm simply not in that frame of mind right now; I think instantly switching from endless days on the open road and nights spent in small-town America, to suddenly being immersed in the bustle of one of the world's greatest cities – it would be a huge culture shock, and I just wouldn't enjoy it.

I point the bike north, following the lakeshore drive with skyscrapers to my left and the choppy waters of the lake crashing onto the beach and against rocks and piers to my right. As the city recedes I pass marinas full of yachts, leafy suburbs, and wide open green countryside once again before pulling in for the night to rest, reflect, and sleep, at a quiet but pleasant little roadside motel.

13th May. 145 miles.

One Of Those Days.

You know those days you sometimes have when absolutely everything goes tits up? The kind of day when you stub your toe as you get out of bed, and that sort of sets the tone for how the rest of the day is going to unfold, all the way through until you finally sit down in the evening and realise that despite all the effort you've expended, you're absolutely no further ahead with anything than you would have been if you hadn't even bothered getting up?

Well here we are, it's Friday the 13th, and whilst I've managed to avoid any toe stubbing and actually succeeded in getting all the way to the bathroom before breaking something, in this case the water glass which shatters into a thousand tiny pieces as it hits the tiles, I've already got a red and stinging left eye as a result of squirting a dollop of shampoo straight into it, and I've spilled hot coffee over my foot. I'm not even bloody dressed yet!

Proceeding with extreme caution, I pack up my things and check out of the motel, successfully avoiding burning the place to the ground in the process.

Having stalled the bike for the first time, which takes quite some doing with such a huge capacity, low revving engine as this, I've set my course north from Chicago as I have a kind of personal pilgrimage to make today. I'm riding a little further up the lake shore, crossing from Illinois into the state of Wisconsin and heading for the city of Milwaukee, noted for the brewing of beer by the likes of Miller and Coors; indeed for many years it wore the crown as the world's leading beer producing city. And much as the production of unimaginable quantities of beer is enough justification in itself, there's another and, in my view at least, even more valid reason for making a special detour to visit this place – which is that it's home to the global headquarters of Harley-Davidson Motorcycles. Having travelled all this way, I feel it would be criminal to pass so close without calling in and having a look around the place where they built the fabulous machine which has just transported me along every single mile of the world's most legendary highway.

I haven't got terribly far to go, so I spend some time calling the kids for a catch up while I take a coffee break at a little roadside diner before setting off again and meandering my way along the quieter roads which hug the shoreline, becoming rather frustrated as the day is gradually spoiled by increasingly damp and unpleasant conditions. The day's catalogue of mishaps gets added to further as I pull into another diner to escape the drizzle and get a bite of lunch. The car park is a mass of puddles, and I choose to ride through the one that's concealing a very large pothole; causing the bike to lurch to a standstill and me to place both feet down firmly into four inches of water.

I eventually arrive at the factory in the middle of the afternoon with rather soggy feet, and park up in what strikes me as a surprisingly empty car park. I suppose the weather isn't very conducive to a nice run out though, and at least I won't have to queue if there aren't many folk around. Climbing the big wide steps to the main entrance doors, I can already see tantalising hints of gleaming chrome sparkling under the spotlights on the other side of the glass. I grasp the polished stainless steel door handle and – it doesn't budge. I try pushing it the other way, but still nothing. Why the hell is the bloody door locked?

Taking a pace backwards in puzzlement and confusion, I look around for the other door which I've obviously not noticed, and what I actually do notice is the sign which reads 'Factory Tours. Daily 10 am to 3 pm.' Oh. Right then. And it's ten past three. All this way just to press my nose against the damp glass and peer inside to see an empty reception desk and a handful of bikes on display. Well isn't that just the way things are going today! What the hell's going to go wrong next? I hardly dare walk back to the bike for fear it might inexplicably topple over or spontaneously combust.

Ok, enough is enough, and I know I'm going to get really pissed off if this shambolic excuse for a day manages to get any worse. It's clearly one of those days that needs bringing to a close and putting out of its misery as soon as possible, and definitely before it gets the chance to find any further opportunities to drive me to the edge of despair.

Retracing my route here, I consider how much further I can face riding through the drab and damp afternoon and where I might stay tonight. It occurs to me that the task of searching out a motel probably carries great potential for another calamity, and so decide there and then just to return to the same place I stayed last night. At least I know how to get there, I know the rooms are ok and that I can get fed nearby, and hopefully they'll have forgiven me for the broken glass in the bathroom.

It certainly hasn't been an auspicious start to the next phase of my adventure; and I sincerely hope it isn't an omen, because there's an awful lot of riding still ahead of me and it won't be much fun if every day delivers a similar catalogue of disasters to today's.

I conclude that the right thing to do is to place today into a metaphorical box, close the lid, and shove it in the back of a dark cupboard. Yesterday was the end of the first adventure, and tomorrow is the start of the second. Today was just the interlude in the middle, so it doesn't count and it won't be allowed to taint the experience. There, problem sorted, mind re-focussed, on with the journey.

14th May. 278 miles.

Back In The Groove.

Today is, thankfully, another day, and a dry and bright morning lifts my spirits back to a more than acceptable level. Dry feet rather help too. I pack up and head south, back along the coastal road to Chicago, and before long I find myself having to stop and strip off a layer as the sun has already gone from being pleasantly warm to a little too hot. Oh yes, this is definitely a big improvement on yesterday already – not that it's very difficult, as the bar was set rather low.

I can't resist stopping at Grant Park again, just to sit for a while with a coffee and take a last long nostalgic look down Route 66 as it sets off through the urban jungle on the first leg of its epic journey to the west coast.

Thoughts and images drift through my mind as I daydream. I see Claudio preening himself as he awaits his next eager adventurer arriving to collect their bike. I hear the hustle and bustle of the non-stop action on The Strip in Las Vegas, and the desolate empty silence of the Mojave Desert. I picture Andrea back at the Bagdad Café, cheerfully welcoming the morning's bus load of trippers; and Johnie serving up another delicious Uranium Burger. I wonder if the dungaree-clad brothers have managed to waddle back down from Sky City yet, and whether the waitress in McClean has finally popped next door to have a look around the museum. The guys from Barnsley must have finished their trip and handed back their massive pickup by now, and Wally and Marilyn will be safely back at home in Michigan. I wonder if the old guy in the bar full of bras is still sitting exactly where I left him – more than likely I suspect. Life goes on for the people of Route 66, and it's been such a great pleasure to share those fleeting moments in time with each and every one of them. I'm sure that, in their minds, I'll be just a vague memory at best by now; but I'm certain that I won't ever forget a single one of them.

A lifetime of memories for sure, but there are still more to be made and it's time to move on. I join Highway 41, the South Lake Shore Drive, which is initially an eight lane freeway whisking me quickly away from central Chicago before narrowing to become a relatively quiet and very beautiful ride through leafy suburbs and a succession of wide open lakeside parks and recreation areas as it leads me down to the southern end of the lake, the point where I shall turn eastwards once more.

At the little community of Robertsdale I branch off

to join Highway 20, another very notable road. It runs for well over 3,000 miles, right across the continent from the Pacific coast in Oregon all the way to Boston, and I'm going to be following it for large parts of the remainder of my journey.

I stop to stretch my legs for a while at the glorious Indiana Dunes State Park; a stunningly beautiful, unspoiled and undeveloped stretch of lakeshore stretching for several miles with wonderful sandy beaches and pleasantly warm water gently lapping at the sand; and all but deserted too. Lake Michigan, as with so many other aspects of America like the deserts I've crossed or the Grand Canyon for example, is another impressive demonstration of how the geography of this nation is on an altogether different scale to what I'm used to. When a Brit like me talks about a 'big lake', we might be referring to Windermere in the Lake District, or perhaps Loch Lomond in Scotland, or Rutland Water further south. But compare the numbers for a moment and you'll get an idea of the difference I'm talking about. Windermere covers an area of about 5.7 square miles, Loch Lomond dwarfs it at 27 square miles, and Rutland Water barely registers at just 4.2. Lake Michigan's surface area is 22,400 square miles; which means Windermere, proudly promoting itself as the largest lake in England, would fit into Lake Michigan nearly four thousand times. Think about that for a minute – it's not four times as big as England's biggest lake, it's four *thousand* times as big. Even more mind-boggling still, Michigan is only the third largest of the Great Lakes (the biggest, Lake Superior, measures in at 31,700 square miles).

This is why, sitting on the beach between the dunes and the water's edge, I don't feel at all like I'm looking out over a lake. In every respect this really is the seaside, the only noticeable difference being that the water isn't salty.

Having spent a while marvelling at the vastness of this inland sea, and very much enjoying feeling the warm sunshine on my skin as I consign yesterday's debacle to the scrapheap of unwanted memories, I continue east a little further before breaking for some lunch at the idyllic little town of New Carlisle, where I sit in the park with a sandwich and watch a kids baseball game. All is well with the world once again.

Passing through the townships of Elkhart and Lagrange, I find myself all of a sudden in the heart of Indiana's Amish country; where the preferred method of transport is still the pony and trap, and the road is filled with lots of identical plain black carriages pulled by matching black horses trotting along with their simply dressed occupants still apparently happily existing in the 19th century. A horse drawn plough working in a field next to the road completes the sense of having travelled back in time, and all around me the beautifully tended houses, farms and fields make the whole area a delight to behold.

They're certainly a very little understood community and, like many others I imagine, my limited knowledge of the Amish stems almost entirely from the Oscar-winning film Witness, starring Harrison Ford as the detective assigned to protect a young Amish boy who's witnessed a murder, and Kelly McGillis as the boy's mother. They're deeply religious people, with an overriding sense of community; they eschew almost all modern technology, and they're not afraid of a bit of hard graft. I think I need to at least do them the service of learning a little more than that!

My route leads on through Angola, which is a good deal prettier than its name suggests, and into what must be some of the most fertile farmland in the country, including a number of small vineyards which are very reminiscent of rural France.

I pass through Toledo and pull in for the night at its near neighbour, Maumee. Flopping onto the bed, I feel a satisfying tiredness and reflect on a good distance covered today, and a significant start made on the second stage of my great adventure.

It feels very different now though. I'm still riding the same bike on the same long journey, but it's just not Route 66 anymore. Is that going to make all the rest of the trip feel like an anti-climax I wonder? I do hope not, because there are a great many miles left to be travelled. It's all in the mind of course, and a question of perspective. In the years to come, if someone asks me about my travels, what will I say? I once rode right across America? Or I once rode Route 66? It'll be the latter, of course, because Route 66 was the main event. As for the rest of the journey across to the east coast, well it's partly about making a complete crossing from the sea on one side to the sea on the other, and of course partly just a case of 'well, seeing as I'm here anyway, I might as well'.

I resolve that I need to reframe the way I think about this. It's very much a two part trip, I always knew it would be; that was part one, and now this is part two, and of course it will feel different. The roads have different names, the landscape is different, the whole look and feel of everything about it is different – not inferior, just different.

I feel better having thought it through and squared it in my head. There'll be plenty of time to look back and think of Route 66, but now is not that time. Now it's time to keep looking ahead, keep riding towards the east coast, and keep living the dream.

15th May. 258 miles.

Through The Rust Belt.

I have a strong feeling that today is going to be one of those days when you've just got to crack on and get through a succession of unattractive places purely in order to reach the good stuff which lies beyond.

Sandusky is my first port of call, billed as the 'best place to live cheaply' in the USA. Now there's more than one way to interpret that description isn't there? Sitting at the southwestern corner of Lake Erie, the town originally gained prominence as a significant trading port; and I'm interested to learn that it was at one time a major stopping off point for refugee slaves waiting to cross the lake in search of freedom and a new life in Canada, and also that ice harvesting was a booming industry here back in the 19th century. I didn't know there was ever such a thing as ice harvesting, but I can see the logic.

Modern day Sandusky is largely given over to recreation, and the fact that it's still very early in the season probably explains why the place is so quiet today. The town's main attraction seems to be the Cedar Point amusement park, with its sizeable collection of rollercoasters; but far bigger overall are the ten or so yacht marinas spread along the shoreline and ranging in size from quite large to absolutely massive. Sitting for a while and looking out over the never ending forest of masts, all rhythmically clanking away as the breeze taps the wire halyards against the aluminium, I idly start the mental arithmetic of 'well if each boat on average is worth maybe 75,000 dollars, and I guess there must be 500 just in this marina, and there are at least ten marinas....' Quickly realising the futility of the exercise, I conclude that it's just a hell of a lot of cash all sitting here tied up to a jetty and not doing anything – apart from bleeding even more cash just for the pleasure of being neatly moored and going no-where.

Moving on, it's a very beautiful drive for fifty miles or so along the lake shore towards Cleveland. Much of the road is lined with trees either side, but it still affords frequent views across the lake. There are lots of expensive looking properties with neatly mani-cured lawns running down to the water's edge, along with occasional little holiday parks and hotels. It would be an absolutely perfect place to live, but only if you never had to visit the city which lies just a little further along the road.

Cleveland is an utterly dreadful and depressing place with badly maintained roads, mind-numbingly endless sets of traffic lights, and suburbs which never seem to end. The city is apparently on the up now, although there's precious little evidence that I can see, as the scars of decades of decline remain all too evident. This was once a truly great industrial city, the epicentre of the mighty steel industry; but gradual shifts in the nature of the global economy saw its prominence level off and begin to decline in the early 1960's, until in 1978 it became the first major American city to default on its federal loans. In simple terms, it went bust; and it takes a long time to get properly back on your feet after that kind of thing happens. In fact it took a whole decade just to climb back out of default. As I ride through the remnants of its past, I wonder whether it might have been best to just wipe it off the map and start afresh.

There's certainly no doubting where the term 'Rust Belt' came from – not just Cleveland, but vast swathes of the Midwest and Northeast are littered with the decaying remnants of a great industrial past; and one of the most striking things you notice as you travel through the region is indeed rust. Right now we're still in that inevitable period of transition, where the towns and cities which came so close to the brink are reinventing themselves, gradually halting and reversing their decline by nurturing new industries like healthcare, tech, and services; yet at the same time they've still got a long way to go in clearing the wastelands of the past.

Finally escaping the interminable succession of

traffic lights and industrial dereliction, I enjoy another brief spell of trundling along with pleasant views over Lake Erie as I cross the state line from Ohio into Pennsylvania, until I reach the outskirts of the city of Erie itself. As I'd expected, it's like Cleveland but a touch smaller, and there's not much else to say about the place.

The day has unfolded much as expected so far, and I note with a wry smile that I have yet to feel the urge to pull my camera from my pocket. But immediately on leaving the city limits of Erie, it's a very different story indeed. The last few miles of Pennsylvania and the first few of New York State are absolutely delightful, and clearly a major wine producing region too. I'd been taken by surprise by a few little fields of vines yesterday, but now I'm riding through what must be hundreds of square miles of grape vines, all growing in their neatly regimented rows and hanging from supporting wires like drunks trying to hold themselves from falling down. It really is extraordinary how suddenly the change comes – you're riding along through urban and suburban sprawl, the end of which is marked almost like a gatehouse by an enormous Walmart Supercentre, and then a hundred yards further on there are fields of vines stretching all the way to the horizon. And they just go on and on, only occasionally interrupted by a few houses here and there, and most of those have even got a few vines growing in the garden. I reckon if you took up every offer of free wine tasting along the roadside, you'd be paralytic before you'd covered five miles.

What promised to be quite a dull day has certainly ended well. And let's face it, you can't have a Grand Canyon every day. The places I've travelled through today haven't been sensational highlights, but that certainly doesn't mean they haven't been interesting or played their own important part in the overall journey; so I'm more than happy with another day on the road as I decide that the pretty little town of Westfield looks like a good place to spend the night.

16th May. 204 miles.

Which Way Is Up?

According to my guide book, there's only one place for the discerning traveller to take breakfast in Westfield, and that's the Main Street Diner.

Sadly I can't add my own personal recommendation of the aforementioned establishment because it's closed today, which is a pity. But no real harm is done, as an equally nice looking café just across the road is open and feeds me well, and I set off in good spirits to seek out and inspect the little community of Chautauqua, which is apparently some kind of preserved utopia of 19th century values and standards. In reality, it looks to me a lot more like a posh housing estate with a fence to keep the riff raff out. It holds no attraction to this itinerant biker, and I suspect the feeling is mutual, so I retrace my tracks back to Westfield, take a sharp right, and thoroughly enjoy the calm and happy feeling of riding unhurriedly along a beautiful lakeshore drive, past yet more vineyards and through a series of quaint little lakeside towns. I'm obviously very relaxed today, because I'm paying absolutely no attention to where I'm going when I arrive in the busy conurbation of Buffalo, and promptly become hopelessly lost.

It takes a little while to solve the puzzle of where I've gone wrong, but eventually I'm back on track and a short while later find myself staring in astonishment across the breathtaking magnificence of the Niagara Falls. Here we go again, nature's back on steroids! The falls are immense, dramatic, powerful; in fact you can give them any extreme adjective you like, and it'll probably fit. They're also surrounded on all sides by development, with hotels, casinos, and viewing towers shoehorned into every last available space, while down below the tourist boats nose their bows cautiously into the billowing spray at the very base of the falls themselves. Despite man's best efforts to take the edge off the rawness of it all, it remains an impressive sight and I enjoy a few hours wandering around finding different angles and views of the cascading walls of water, accompanied by the ever present roar and the fine mist which both fill the air.

Niagara Falls isn't actually one big waterfall, but is divided into three sections thanks to two small islands in the Niagara River right where it drops 180 feet over a cliff edge, and the three falls all have their own names; Horseshoe Falls is the largest, followed by the American Falls and the relatively tiny Bridal Veil Falls. The amount of water plunging over this lot is quite staggering – obviously it varies a fair amount according to the time of year or how much water is being diverted for generating hydro-electricity, but typically when you gaze in wonder at the mighty power of these falls, you're watching six million cubic feet of water dropping over the edge every minute. If you want some sort of context for that, then it's roughly three full size Olympic swimming pools in the time it takes you to say 'Niagara Falls', and when the river rises to full flood conditions then you're looking at nearly three times that.

One peculiar detail, which makes me feel rather foolish, is that the falls flow in the opposite direction to that which I had, for some strange reason, expected. What made me imagine that they would flow north to south, rather than south to north, I wonder? Well north is 'up' and south is 'down', isn't it? I guess it's the same kind of misguided logic that makes you think walking from John O'Groats to Land's End must be easier than going the other way, simply because you're travelling from top to bottom and it must therefore be downhill. Anyway, in the interests of clarity, let me confirm once and for all that the water flows in a northerly direction over the falls; and if I hang around in this mist pondering which way is up for much longer then I'm going to end up wetter than an otter's pocket.

The falls, or rather the Niagara River which connects lakes Erie and Ontario and falls over the falls in between the two, also happens to serve as the border between the United States and Canada; and so after climbing back aboard the bike and crossing the bridge with a final view of the falls, I pass through the customs post and stop at an exchange booth to change the small amount of cash I have left in my pocket. It transpires that seventeen US dollars is equal to seventeen Canadian dollars, so I'm not quite sure why the exercise was entirely necessary, save for the preservation of national pride and identity of course.

A detour into Canada has, up until a couple of days ago, only been loosely in my mind as an option to be taken if it seems that the time is available. But a quick calculation (on the back of a beermat again) carried out last night suggests that there is indeed plenty of time, so here we go – and I refer again to my musings on the benefits of not having a fixed plan or itinerary when embarking on this kind of journey.

Once through customs and away from Niagara Falls, I take the motorway which follows the shore of Lake Ontario around its western end towards the gleaming spires of Toronto and its dominant landmark, the 550 metre high slender spike with what looks like a doughnut skewered on it, and which is actually known as the CN Tower. CN, by the way, stands for Canadian National, the railway company which built it.

The rules are different now; I'm not following the course of a legendary old road, and so taking motorways isn't cheating or risking missing out the good bits. I've done the main thing I came here to do, and now it's a case of seeing and experiencing as much as I possibly can in the two weeks remaining between now and the only other thing which is actually booked and set in stone, namely my flight home.

An hour and a half later I'm luxuriating in a deep hot bathtub in the downtown Marriot Hotel, having justified the expense mainly on the basis of its very useful facility of secure underground parking for the bike, as well as the friendly doorman who's promised to keep a close eye on it for me.

I'm not generally one for big cities, but I'm immediately taken with Toronto. It doesn't seem to have quite the usual levels of noise and bustle and hassle. Heading out in search of food and drink, the area of downtown immediately surrounding me is all towering steel and glass skyscrapers as you look upwards from leafy squares and pedestrianised areas filled with chic and expensive shops and restaurants. I haven't wandered far when a familiar and hugely exciting sign hanging outside a bar catches my eye. Fullers London Pride. Wow, here in Toronto, who'd have thought. For those who might not know (although the name kind of gives it away) London Pride is an English beer, brewed by Fullers, and it's very nice indeed. One slight issue though – once the barman has pulled the pint (yes, it's hand pumped), he then carefully adorns the rim of the glass with a generous slice of lime before placing it on the bar in front of me. I stare blankly, speechless and shocked, at this appalling crime committed in full public view. This is the equivalent of serving a Jack Daniels on ice with a cherry, an olive, and a cocktail umbrella shoved in it; or steak and chips with a dollop of custard on top. It just isn't done, and I'm completely at a loss as to how anyone ever thought it was an appropriate thing to do. With as much tact and diplomacy as I can muster, which isn't very much, I make it clear that the lime isn't particularly to my taste and remove it quickly before the beer gets polluted any further.

Leaving aside this gross act of sacrilege, a few lime-free pints of London Pride are exactly what I need to pour down my throat this evening, and a fairly decent meal is served up to complement them so my requirements are fully satisfied and I eventually slide into bed feeling thoroughly well fed as well as a little tipsy.

17th May. 128 miles.

You Can't Afford It.

I begin the day with a little exploration of downtown Toronto, soaking up the sights and sounds of what strikes me as a very cool city; although I'm surprised to see that it does appear to have quite a significant vagrancy problem. There were no beggars on the streets or people in sleeping bags in doorways as I walked around last night, so they must have all taken up their positions later in the evening; and as most of the shops haven't opened just yet they're still making the most of the last few minutes before they get moved on.

I happen across a little internet café, which seems to be missing a trick by not actually serving coffee, and take the opportunity to send a couple of emails home (it will be a few more years yet before we simply do this with our smartphones).

I find a pavement café more deserving of the title, and after a nice long cappuccino and a very delicious pastry, and having watched the city gradually wind up to full operating speed, I load up the bike, bid Toronto farewell, and head east once more.

I'm following Highway 2, as I will be all day, which at the moment is running parallel with the northern shore of Lake Ontario but a mile or two inland. As with Route 66, this was once the main road but is now pleasantly traffic free thanks to the newer dual carriageway which has taken over the main burden, and has been built far enough away from the old road so as not to bother me with its presence. Once I'm completely clear of the sprawl of the city, the landscape soon begins to hint that this is a really big country. There's an awful lot of open countryside and forest with not much habitation or other sign of human existence to interrupt it, especially when you bear in mind that this is the crowded part – there's another two thousand miles or so of land to the north of me with hardly anybody in it at all.

After a couple of hours trundling along the road, with the ever-reliable engine booming out its relentless rhythm, I break for lunch in the delightful little town of Port Hope, with its beautifully preserved 19th century architecture and immaculately kept streets. It's been lucky to escape being ruined in the name of progress, and the locals are clearly very determined to keep it that way. I'm surprised to find though that the actual port itself, such as it is, is entirely commercial; just a tiny little dock with very little going on, surrounded by a few small industrial buildings. There's not a pleasure boat of any description to be found, which is weird. A gorgeous town, built right on the shore of a beautiful lake, and nobody seems to have a boat.

After Port Hope the road continues with its rather frustrating habit of following the lake shore, but not closely enough that you can actually see the water. I don't know what the engineer who planned it was thinking, but he certainly didn't have enough of a visionary mindset to be able to foresee the popularity of the scenic lake shore drive.

Towards the end of the afternoon I stop for a coffee in the little township of Brighton; and I take a quick look at the map to see where I might head next, and whether I can do something about this lamentable lack of lake views. It's interesting to see that I've been on the road for most of the day already, and moving at a reasonably good pace, and yet I've succeeded merely in travelling about half the length of a lake. That doesn't happen where I come from, unless you're on foot and in no hurry.

A detour to the south onto some smaller roads looks like a promising option, and sure enough it's not too long before I'm finally rewarded with the full lake shore experience rather than just occasional snatched glimpses through the trees.

The time is getting on now though, and my luck appears to be in as the Wellington Willows bed and breakfast presents itself by the side of the road with more or less perfect timing. It's early evening already and accommodation seems to be a bit thin on the ground around this neck of the woods; and in any case it looks immaculately kept and really rather nice. As I pull into the drive the proprietor approaches, rather cautiously I sense, from the far end of the garden where I suspect he has been attending to a couple of blades of grass which have been discovered growing at slightly the wrong angle, or a rogue weed ruining an otherwise perfect flower bed.

I'm in the process of loosening the buckle on my helmet ready to introduce myself and enquire whether there's a room available, when without waiting he opens the conversation with 'I don't think you can afford it son.' And there was me anticipating something more along the lines of 'Hey, it's been a beautiful day for a ride; so are you looking for a room?' I opt to ignore the clear hint that I should keep my helmet on and bugger off, and instead respond perfectly calmly with 'Well that depends on how much it is.'

'It's gotta be at least sixty dollars.'

'Ok, well how about we call it sixty dollars then?'

'Well come on in then, there's actually no one else here tonight so I'll show you to the big room at the front; and here, bring your bike over to the garage and we'll get it under cover and locked up safe.'

This is more than a little bizarre! Does he test all potential guests in the same way I wonder? Not wishing to break the spell, I go with it and it gets even better. My bedroom can be accurately described as many things, including vast, spotlessly clean, immaculately decorated, warm and cosy, with the most divinely comfortable four poster bed and a gleaming en-suite bathroom.

Stick with me here, as it now gets better still. On his way out of the room, Ron (as he has now introduced himself) tells me to pop my laundry in a pile in the corner before I go out, and he'll get it washed and dried for me. For a moment I think he must be referring to the bed linen and towels when I leave in the morning; but no, he really is offering to wash my pants and socks, and in the full knowledge that I am travelling by motorbike and therefore unlikely to be in a high state of cleanliness.

Still wondering quite when I'm going to wake from this rather bizarre dream, I head out (having duly left my laundry ready for housekeeping) and wander along the road into Wellington for some beer and food. Choice is limited but perfectly good, and it's a very pleasant little town to stroll through on a sunny evening. I can only conclude that Ron's initial 'greeting' must have been based on a specific set of assumptions about bikers; but as I removed my helmet to reveal no long dirty beard, then removed my jacket to reveal no oily t-shirt and no tattoos, and of course spoke in a middle class English accent, his perception of me and my acceptability as a guest rapidly changed for the better. If that's what it was, then I'm happy to forgive his prejudices and pleased that he didn't completely judge the book by its cover.

Returning to the Willows, I now find that Ron has the whisky bottle and two glasses sitting ready on the table. I'm rather ashamed to confess to a fleeting, and as it transpires unfounded, suspicion that Ron's ever increasing levels of friendliness and hospitality may have an ulterior motive, particularly as there continues to be absolutely no evidence of the existence of a female member of the household. A couple of whiskies on the rocks and the revelation that Ron's wife, Linda, is away visiting friends leads to a most enjoyable and relaxing remainder of the evening chatting away with him about life, the universe, and everything in between. What an exceptionally nice bloke, thanks Ron.

18th May. 255 miles.

My Damn Sexy Accent.

I wake to glorious sunshine and the rather worrying news that Mum now needs an operation, which is scheduled for tomorrow. There's nothing I can do beyond wait and hope for the best of course, so it's a case of fingers crossed and press on. I do find it hard though, as I think most people do, when the natural instinct is to do everything you possibly can to help and make things better; but circumstances or, in this case, distance render you completely powerless to act.

Ron serves up an absolutely splendid breakfast, thus confirming his place as the best host of the entire journey, and cheerily sends me and my clean underwear on our way into a beautifully sunny, yet still refreshingly cool, morning. I pass through the charming little town of Picton, much of which bears a very English appearance, before arriving at Glenora where a short ferry crossing means a pleasantly relaxing few minutes of sitting in the sun watching the little boat make its way slowly back from the far bank. I love these little places with local ferries; there are quite a few around the UK too, and they inevitably lead to a slower and much more relaxed pace of life. There's really no point trying to be in a rush to get anywhere when you know you're going to have to stop and wait for half an hour for the boat to arrive.

Disembarking on the other side, the road continues right along the lake shore towards Kingston. It's a perfect day and the lake's surface is as smooth as a sheet of glass as I ride along just yards from the water; the banks a carpet of lush green grass and lovely wild flowers. Whoever laid out this stretch of road clearly *did* get the memo about scenic drives, as there are frequent little gravelled areas to pull in, sit down on a perfectly placed wooden bench, and while away a few minutes just gazing out over the vast inland sea in front of you.

The city of Kingston effectively marks the point where Lake Ontario turns into the mighty St. Lawrence River as it heads off towards Montreal, then Quebec, and finally into the Atlantic Ocean; and a few miles later I take a detour to the south and onto the Thousand Islands Parkway. This area actually consists of closer to two thousand islands, and is indeed the birthplace of that sickly pink salad dressing which so often accompanies a few limp lettuce leaves and a handful of defrosted prawns. The road makes for a staggeringly beautiful final few miles of my excursion into Canada as it weaves its way along the tree covered shoreline, crossing inlets, skirting bays, and delivering an endless stream of breathtaking views over the water to the archipelago of islands scattered along this six mile wide stretch of river.

Following a fairly self-explanatory sign which announces 'Bridge to USA', I turn south once again and cross the river, which also doubles as the border, back into New York State. It's by no means the end of the lake for me just yet though, and I continue hugging its eastern shoreline as I follow the scenic route to Oswego where I make a rather overdue stop for morning coffee. The waitress is delightful; charming with a sharp inquiring mind and fascinated by some of the details of my trip. We share a very enjoyable chat for an hour, as other customers are pretty thin on the ground, and she excels herself further still by announcing that the coffee is on the house because, as she puts it, I have a 'damn sexy accent'.

It seems that the 'yard sale' is a popular means of disposing of one's rubbish in the many small lakeside communities around here, as I frequently pass home-made signs advertising the mounds of worn out domestic paraphernalia which can be seen laid out on tables on the lawns and in the driveways. I notice one particularly honest and realistic resident has erected a very large sign which bears just the single word 'CRAP' in big black spray painted letters. It's a concept which hasn't really caught on in the UK, where we dutifully drive all our rubbish to the local waste disposal centre on a Sunday morning. The American approach might leave the neighbourhood looking a little untidy in places, but why go to all the bother of getting rid of your rubbish when you can just plonk it on the drive and wait for someone else to take it away for you – and occasionally even give you a couple of dollars for it.

A little beyond Oswego I finally leave Lake Ontario behind me and head south towards Geneva on Highway 14. I've been following the shores of this lake for well over 400 miles now, and I'm still a long way short of completing a full circumnavigation which would require me to carry on for another hundred miles or so until I arrived back at Niagara Falls.

Riding now through endless orchards with neatly ordered trees laden and dripping with sweet scented blossom, it's very clear that apples are the crop of choice in this particular area. Geneva seems a pleasant spot, and I wonder what the connection is with its better known namesake which sits astride the border between France and Switzerland. Apart from the fact that they're both situated at the head of beautiful lakes, I can't find any information as to what the link may be.

Re-joining Highway 20, the coast to coast artery which accounts for a large portion of this second phase of the journey, it's a short ride to the town of Seneca Falls at the heart of the Finger Lakes region, and it seems like a sufficiently attractive spot to spend the night. It takes only a few minutes to find myself some comfortable lodgings, and after an entirely fruitless search for the waterfalls which I presumed must have given the place its name, but which clearly did not as there are none to be found, I spend a relaxing evening with a few beers and a guidebook, swotting up on all the delights which the Finger Lakes and surrounding countryside have to offer the passing traveller.

Apparently there are 11 lakes in the region, all running roughly north-south and formed by glacial activity. Their layout rather reminded early map makers of human fingers, and the nickname stuck. I never realised that early map makers were distinguished by the peculiar characteristic of having eleven fingers, but there you go. If you want to define the area with one single word, then that word would have to be 'wine'. And if you allowed it an extra adjective, then you could add 'serene'. Despite the miles of apple orchards I've just travelled through, it's still the grape which reigns supreme. This is New York State's largest wine producing region, with over one hundred wineries and vineyards growing a wide variety of grapes, many of them of French and German origin, and a good number of them are open to visitors. Roll on tomorrow!

Doug's Fish Fry.

I'm in the midst of a stunningly beautiful land-scape of forests, lakes, and vineyards, and I have time in hand, so a gentle day of sightseeing seems like a thoroughly good plan.

I set off southwards from Seneca Falls, enjoying a terrific ride along Highway 89 which follows the west-ern shore of Cayuga Lake. It's a perfect stretch of road for this bike, with a lovely smooth surface and end-lessly long sweeping curves which are an absolute joy to ride. On any other kind of bike it might seem a bit too straight, but as I think I may have mentioned before – Harley's don't do tight bends. Lean them over far enough to take a moderate bend at a decent pace, and you'll be scraping the exhausts or the foot pegs on the tarmac before you know it. I'm reminded of when I first bought my bike, when I made the mistake of be-lieving the marketing hype in the brochure which said something about the frame geometry making it cap-able of 'really pegging the bends'. How was I to know it was complete bullshit? I had neither the knowledge nor the experience to make comparisons. But hey, don't slate Harleys for being rubbish at corners, just accept that they don't do that and appreciate what they do do.

As enjoyable as the ride is turning out to be, it isn't too long before the lure of the grape proves too strong to resist; so about half way down the length of the lake I follow a promising looking signpost and turn into a little side road which runs down to the shore and leads me to the Sheldrake Point Winery. Here I spend a perfect hour sipping a truly excellent glass of Riesling, sitting on a picnic bench on the neatly tended lawns which roll down to the water's edge. If tranquillity and beauty is your thing, then it doesn't get much better to be honest. A crystal clear lake surrounded by heavily wooded rolling hills, the gentlest of breezes just rippling the water's surface, and the bright spring sunshine bringing out the full intensity of the colours. I could happily get slowly sozzled and snooze away the rest of the day right here.

A little further down the road I come across the rather curious sight of an Amish retail outlet – not something I would have imagined would exist, given the Amish rejection of pretty much all things commercial. It seems worthy of further investigation but proves to be somewhat disappointing. I do admire some of the superb outdoor furniture which is on sale, but there's an awful lot of horribly tacky bits and bobs too.

After the disappointment of the Amish retail opportunity, perfection is once again the order of the day in the form of the Taughannock Falls, an immaculately proportioned waterfall cascading without interruption for 215 feet into a plunge pool below which is so perfectly circular that it seems to have been gouged out of the rock by a giant ice cream scoop. Parking areas and viewpoints and waymarked trails make it obvious that it's a very popular tourist spot, as indeed it should be because it's wonderful, and yet I seem to have the whole place completely to myself this morning. I take advantage of the unexpected solitude by setting up the camera to get a well framed shot without the hassle of trying to find a gap in the people – you know the frustration when you set the timer, click the shutter, dash into position, and some bloody kid with an ice cream wanders into the frame right at the critical moment!

Ithaca marks the southern tip of the lake, and I turn back northwards on Highway 34 which weaves its way through a rolling landscape of cultivated arable land and many thousands of acres of deciduous forest. If anything, the riding is even better than this morning, as the road snakes its way through the undulating countryside between the Cayuga and Owasco lakes.

At the town of Auburn I'm reunited with Highway 20 just fifteen miles from where I started the day in Seneca Falls, and I turn east once more towards Skaneateles (pronounced, rather charmingly, 'skinny atlas') which proves to be a picture perfect lakeside resort at the head of its namesake lake. It's a rather genteel tourist hotspot so I easily find a very nice and comfortable guesthouse quite close to the centre of town, and with it still being early in the season the price isn't too extortionate.

I chance upon the excellent Doug's Fish Fry during my search for evening sustenance, and am treated to simple and traditional fish and chips, just the way it should be and of a quality I reckon is unmatched, anywhere. I suppose that might be something of a sacrilegious statement coming from an Englishman, but credit where it's due, and I'm sticking to my assertion. In addition to serving superb fayre wrapped in real newspaper, Doug also likes to hand out car stickers to his customers which they are then duty bound to photograph in exotic locations around the world before posting the picture back to him for display on the restaurant walls. They're all there of course - Doug's Fish Fry at the Sydney Opera House, Doug's Fish Fry at Tower Bridge in London, Doug's Fish Fry in Red Square, Moscow, and Doug's Fish Fry on the Great Wall of China. I duly take a sticker with me, which it turns out I shall eventually photograph at Colditz Castle, the famous second world war prison in Germany, a year or so hence. It's not a prison anymore by the way, it's a youth hostel – so probably little different in terms of facilities.

It eat my delicious supper sitting on a park bench and watching a lake steamer gliding slowly and silently towards the pier. The scene is utterly delightful, peaceful, calm, and tranquil. I bet it's been a while since the local doctor had to treat anyone suffering from stress.

A fine evening continues with several beers too many in the company some very friendly locals at Moris's Bar. They're on fine form and getting stuck into a good session, but the general nature of the place and its clientele means the atmosphere isn't rowdy, just jovial and lively with lots of good natured banter. It's been a great day, I've got good company, I'm in a good mood, and I end up getting thoroughly hammered - although the biggest highlight of the day comes just as I'm collapsing semi-comatose into bed, with the news that Mum's operation appears to have gone well and she is now fully awake and in good spirits.

Speaking of locals, I've been noticing over the last few days an increasing number of people commenting on the bike's Californian license plate, and it seems that my trip is widely regarded as a fairly major achievement. Crossing a country doesn't feel like a big deal when you come from a nation in which the feat can be accomplished in a single day by bicycle, but of course America is a continent rather than just a country and an awful lot of people who live on one side have never been to the other, and many who live in the middle have never been to either side. They could though, if they wanted to.

Here's something to ponder. Did you know that

fewer than half the population of America actually possesses a passport? I think to most Europeans, that must be a pretty amazing statistic. But I realise that when you live in a country this big, and with this much variety in its landscapes and it's climate, then you can quite easily enjoy a lifetime's worth of holidays within the borders of your own country and still never visit the same place twice. I get that. What I don't get is the people who spend that lifetime almost exclusively within their own state, or even county. Such a waste, but I suppose I shouldn't judge. If they're happy keeping the boundaries of their world so close, if it maybe makes them feel safe and secure, then that's their choice to make and it's not my place to preach to them.

Taughannock Falls.

20th May. 211 miles.

Reflecting In New York State.

Although I covered more than a hundred miles yesterday, I hardly moved an inch eastwards; so today it's back onto Highway 20 to clock up a few more miles towards the Atlantic seaboard and journey's end.

It's a glorious warm and sunny day once again, and the road is a gently sweeping rollercoaster through heavily forested hills and wide river valleys, dipping and rising through sleepy villages and hundreds upon hundreds of square miles of unspoiled woodland and occasional orchards. Everyone's heard about 'New England in the fall', and although I'm not quite in New England yet, because it officially starts a few miles further ahead when I cross into Massachusetts, and although it's spring rather than fall, I can easily imagine how incredible the colours of this kaleidoscope of trees must look when their leaves begin to take on the oranges and browns of autumn. We get the same autumn shades in England of course, but it's the sheer size of the American landscape that sets it apart. Whereas we Brits might take a trip out to admire a small area of beautiful woodland, and there are certainly plenty of them, here you can drive through it continually for hundreds of miles.

I take a detour around Otsego Lake and through the village of Cooperstown, which announces itself as the home of the National Baseball Hall of Fame Museum. I always find the differing approaches and attitudes of the British and the Americans towards this game quite intriguing, and indeed amusing. Baseball is the national sport of the USA, and so it's deadly serious and incredibly important. In Britain, we call the game Rounders, and it's rarely played by anyone apart from schoolkids, except perhaps for a bit of fun by a group of friends in the park. The idea of Rounders being a major professional sport seems quite ludicrous to us, and yet there is virtually no difference whatsoever between the two disciplines. Funny old things, cultural differences, aren't they? You won't be surprised to learn that I don't take the time to visit the museum.

Riding back up the east side of the lake, I pull in to have a look at Glimmerglass State Park, attracted primarily by its wonderful sounding name. It turns out that Otsego Lake was referred to as Glimmerglass by the author James Fenimore Cooper, of 'Last of the Mohicans' fame. It's a nice enough spot with camping areas and forest trails and a lovely little stretch of beach; but it's not sensational by American standards, so after a short exploration and taking advantage of the excellent toilet facilities I head on up the road.

I'm travelling quite aimlessly today, aware that time is in my favour and enjoying being able to explore wherever the mood takes me without any kind of pressure of a deadline to meet. And so when I join Highway 20 once more, it's only a couple of hundred yards before I divert again onto an attractive looking side road in the hope that I might turn up an alternative to the typical main road diner.

Sure enough, within just a few minutes I'm sitting on a park bench eating a leisurely lunch and watching the world go by in the quiet little village of Cherry Valley, reflecting on how pleasantly relaxing and slow paced the trip has become over recent days. It's very much been transformed from a road trip into an extended bit of 'me time', just meandering gently in the right general direction and with a great sense of inner satisfaction at having achieved something worthwhile, and I'm happy to ease back the pace as I near the end and finally reward myself with a few days off the bike altogether. Having said all that, I know damn well that as soon as I stop moving it'll take about half a day before I'm restless again.

So what exactly is it that I've achieved, anyway? Fair enough, I've travelled Route 66 from end to end on a Harley, which most people would probably agree is a pretty cool thing to do. And then I've carried on and made the thing even bigger by adding this extra stage and making it a complete coast to coast trip too. But it's not difficult is it? It's not exactly a great feat of human endeavour or anything like that. In essence, all you have to do is point the bike in the right direction and sit there admiring the view; and if you repeat that for enough days in succession then you can't fail to get to the other end.

The real source of the sense of achievement, I conclude after much pondering, is not the bit which you can trace on a map, or relive through the memories or the photographs, but the bit which nobody can see – the bit inside which made me stop dreaming and start doing, the bit which ignored all the perfectly valid reasons why I couldn't or shouldn't do something like this, and replaced them with a simple 'hell, why not?' In a nutshell, I suppose the achievement is how it makes me feel to have done it.

I frequently receive emails from people all over the world who've seen pictures or read snippets about the trip, and they invariably go something like 'I'm so envious as I've always wanted to do something like this, but...' (and here you may insert any self-created excuse you wish). I also see countless alpha males beating their chests as they recount tales of their great adventures to everyone within earshot, whether they're interested or not; or boasting about their feats of athletic heroism, their personal best times and the like; and I don't believe I belong in either of these camps. I set out on this adventure because the idea fascinated me and it seemed as though it would be an amazing experience, a kind of extreme personal retreat. And what I've discovered as the trip has unfolded is that it has also been a journey of discovering myself and growing my understanding of both me and the world around me. In turn, I hope it might enable me to inspire at least a few other people to take the same leap of faith, and in so doing to expand their own horizons and find a deeper sense of fulfilment too.

If the point of the whole exercise was to prove anything, then it was only myself that I wanted to prove it to – and indeed I think I have. Of course, I'll happily recount the tale and show the photos to anyone who is interested to hear about it, but I'll be stopping short of forcing it upon anyone who will listen – willingly or otherwise - because it has been, fundamentally, a personal thing and I've done it purely for me.

This in turn brings me to another realisation - that I've discovered the fundamental difference between travelling with company and travelling alone. This is the first big journey I've undertaken on my own, and it's so completely different when you don't have anyone else to think about. Solo travel, I realise, opens up a whole world of self-discovery. It provides the time and space to think and to learn, and now that I've experienced it I can't recommend it highly enough. It's given me the time to write a diary, it's enabled me to stop on a whim and explore places that caught my eye without having to first catch another person's attention and ask if they fancy stopping too. It's also made it much easier to engage with the people that I've met along the way, as there isn't the barrier of a group surrounding me.

Drifting back to the here and now, I find that I've spent more than two hours sitting on this bench in fine Forrest Gump style, pondering the meaning of life and all that stuff – albeit without boring the pants off some unfortunate stranger sitting next to me. I swing back into the saddle and cover a good few miles through the remainder of the afternoon, eventually stopping for a coffee next to the Hudson River in the very pleasant city of Albany where I consult the map to work out a suitable looking destination for the night.

You'd think that New York City would be the capital of New York State wouldn't you? But it isn't, it's Albany, which strikes me as slightly peculiar logic, especially when you consider how it's modest population of just a hundred thousand people compares with NYC's whopping eight and a half million.

I reckon another hour on the road will be enough for today, which makes the town of Pittsfield stand out on the map as the obvious spot to head for. That'll take me just over the state line into Massachusetts, the final state of my journey, setting me up nicely for the last leg.

Pittsfield turns out to be a lovely town; big enough to have everything you need including plenty of options for accommodation, yet small enough to feel friendly and welcoming. Once I'm settled into a comfortable bed and breakfast I head out to explore the centre of town, and over a delicious seafood dinner I get chatting with David and Sylvia, a lovely couple who before long have invited me to come along and join them for a day or two at their caravan in Vermont. This kind of friendliness toward complete strangers does seem to happen more in America than I've ever come across in the UK, although I wonder whether it's because here I'm a bit of a novelty, whereas at home in normal life I'm just another bloke.

They're in the middle of a leisurely few days' break and just meandering around the area, and are genuinely interested to learn more about England and the English. Sylvia enthusiastically tells me about how they even chose what she describes as a 'popular and traditional English name' for their son. He's called Bronson. I smile that 'oh how lovely, yes what an excellent choice' smile, not having the heart to reveal that I've never actually encountered, or even heard of, anyone called Bronson before. I look into it a little later and discover that it is indeed a name of old English origin, albeit an extremely rare one, meaning 'son of brown-haired one'. Neither Sylvia nor David has brown hair.

Time and distance dictate that a visit to Vermont isn't an option, which I feel is a pity, but it's a very nice gesture nonetheless.

21st May. 301 miles.

Strange Behaviour At The Bar.

Although I awake to a beautifully bright and sunny day, the forecast makes it abundantly clear that it isn't going to last very long; so I begin with a few miles of scenic delights to make the most of the sunshine by exploring the area around and to the east of Pittsfield known as The Berkshires.

Heading south for a short while to start with, I'm travelling through New England at its very best, with rolling hills and tranquil river valleys covered with unspoiled deciduous forests stretching for as far as the eye can see. I simply can't count how many subtly different shades of green make up this gentle and serene landscape. Naturally enough, the region's proximity to the huge metropolitan centres of New York City and Boston make it a highly popular recreational area, with countless miles of hiking trails along with a thriving arts scene and several annual festivals to choose from. It would certainly take a great deal of time to tick off all the activities and photo opportunities on offer; and of course for those city dwellers lucky enough to have a few million spare, it's a great place to own a holiday retreat.

Looping back to the north, I bid a final farewell to Highway 20 which has guided me for the last few days, and join Highway 2 at Williamstown to head east along what's known as the Mohawk Trail. Originally an Indian trading route connecting the tribes of the Atlantic coast with their neighbours in upper New York State and far beyond; the Trail today is a designated 'scenic route' of stunning beauty through the glorious landscape of western Massachusetts, running for sixty miles of so from Williamstown to Westminster and the beginnings of the urban sprawl surrounding Boston.

Riding along at an easy pace, I find myself thinking about the huge contrasts between this part of the North American continent and all the other different areas of the country which I've travelled through. I'm currently in the area known as the Eastern Seaboard, which the early English settlers were extremely pleased to discover looked rather like home, except quite a lot bigger; and it's a very pleasant, green, easy land to live in. It's little wonder they liked it and decided to stay; but of course over time some of them got itchy feet and a bit curious, so they started to explore a little further into what's generally referred to as the Midwest. Here the land was still pretty green on the whole, still perfectly fertile, but just not quite so perfect as the east. Still, it was free land for the taking (as long as you were prepared to chase the Indians off), and so they took it and they settled it and began to farm and build towns.

Next in this gradual westward expansion came the Great Plains, and they really were different. These seemingly endless flatlands were vast and empty, and although there was hardly a tree to be seen and the grass certainly didn't grow anywhere near as green, there was just so much of it sitting there waiting to be claimed that it seemed a shame not to. Again, there was the slight issue of indigenous Indian tribes to be dealt with, but these white pioneers weren't to be put off by such trivial inconveniences.

And finally they came to the West; and when you see the landscape they'd left behind in the East, it's little wonder it was soon nicknamed the Wild West. By comparison, this place was just bonkers! All dry barren deserts and other-worldly rock formations; you had to be tough to survive here, let alone prosper, and that in turn meant it attracted more of the, shall we say, 'hardier' element of society who were capable of handling the brutal landscape but also quite partial to a bit of brawling, shooting, wild living and general lawlessness.

Back to the here and now, and I'm nearing the outskirts of Boston; the sunshine has long gone, and the gathering clouds are becoming increasingly dark and threatening. I ponder the options, and with the assistance of a motorway to shorten the potential discomfort and a what-the-hell attitude, I decide to press on to Cape Cod rather than stopping too early and having to spend the night in some drab motel overlooking a motorway intersection. Spots of rain and a rapidly strengthening wind make the next few miles a little less comfortable, but the worst of the weather holds off for a surprisingly long time.

When it does arrive, though, it clearly means business; and by the time I reach the bridge over the canal which marks the beginning of the cape I find that my feet and lower legs are so numb with cold and wet that it's a struggle to work the gear shift lever properly. This is no time for mucking about, so I quickly turn off the motorway and take the old road to the little town of Sandwich in search of lodgings. I've no interest in being picky and choosy now, I just need to collapse into the first place which presents itself and looks like it might be somewhere near my budget. The Earl of Sandwich Motel fits the bill, and within a few short minutes I'm immensely thankful at finding myself with a deep luxurious bath and a huge four poster bed complete with two mattresses, one on top of the other.

Just in case you're wondering what the connection is with the thing you eat for lunch, well it goes roughly like this: Sandwich is an ancient port on the coast of south east England, which this town is named after, and the 4th Earl of Sandwich was a keen gambler who didn't like to break away from his favourite activity just to waste valuable time sitting at the dining table and eating, so he asked his butler to stick a bit of meat between a couple of slices of bread which he could then stuff down his throat while he carried on with the gambling.

It certainly isn't a night for going out and exploring the town, and the motel's bar and restaurant seem to be more than pleasant enough in any case, so I stay firmly put and leave the rain and wind to lash at the windows while I stay warm and dry inside.

After a good slap up meal, I take up position on a stool at the end of the bar, and am soon engaged in conversation by the bloke next to me who says he's overheard my English accent and introduces himself as George. Very much like me when I'm back at home, George is a travelling salesman who's staying at the motel for a couple of nights while visiting customers in the area. Probably in his late 40's, he seems a nice easy going type, and unlike a lot of salesmen, he talks *with* you rather than *at* you. We've been chatting for the best part of an hour, starting with the weather and where I'm from, where he's from, and progressing through different parts of my journey, to the point when he asks where I'm heading next. I reply that I'm intending to finish off my journey by spending a few days just relaxing in Provincetown, at the very tip of Cape Cod. He immediately stops talking, his brow furrows and his eyes narrow ever so slightly, and he moves his stool a few inches further away, turning his attention elsewhere and before long wandering off to the opposite side of the room.

I'm completely baffled by this, not to say a little put out, at least for the time being. It will take until tomorrow for me to realise the underlying reason behind what just happened.

22nd May. 98 miles.

Tossing The Pebble.

I can smell the sea, and I can see it, and all around are seaside towns and villages with names like Falmouth, Yarmouth, Chatham, Harwich, and Truro. There's no disguising where the folk who discovered and settled this part of the world came from. It's a funny thing about a significant number of Brits, the way they travel to foreign climes and then set about trying to make them as much like home as possible. Why can't they be more inclined to expand their minds and experiences by accepting and absorbing new and different cultures? But no, send 'em off to Benidorm and they'll be searching out the nearest English bar the minute they're off the plane. Paella? Tapas? No thanks, they'll have steak pie and chips every time! As for me, well ok I'll hold my hand up guilty as charged over getting excited about that pint of London Pride back in Toronto, but in general I do think that travel is all about discovery and that includes eating and drinking whatever it is the locals do – unless of course they've got a bit of a thing for rotten fish or some such 'delicacy' (sorry Norway). Anyway, the place names are all a bit English, but thankfully that's as far as it goes.

The feeling of achievement and satisfaction is deep and profound as I savour the last few miles, taking the scenic route through Hyannis (where I make an idiot of myself by arriving at a crossroads in the centre of town and turning the wrong way along the one-way main street, to the great consternation of a few animated pedestrians) to Chatham which sits at the very south eastern tip of the cape, proudly sporting a picture perfect lighthouse.

Here I stand and relish my first uninterrupted view of the Atlantic Ocean, and it's an intensely private, thoughtful and contemplative moment. Around me, the deep blue water curls into foamy white surf breaking onto pristine golden sand. The place is remote, wild, utterly serene, and completely deserted. It almost feels as though the world has made a conscious effort to provide me with this space to mark the end of my journey with the respect it deserves.

This is as far east as I will get, as Cape Cod curls back inwards slightly like a beckoning finger as it extends northwards from here; so it feels like a very significant moment and I'm glad to be able to enjoy it in peace, with the only sounds being the breaking waves and the coarse dune grasses rustling in the wind.

I gaze for a long time out across the endless expanse of the ocean to the horizon. If I were to travel precisely due east from here, I wouldn't touch dry land until reaching the city of Viana do Castelo on the northern coast of Portugal, and that's quite a long way away. A little over three thousand miles, to be more precise; although when I think about it, it's not much further than it is back in the other direction to Los Angeles where it all began a few weeks ago, and that's measuring it as the crow flies. I've travelled a little further than the average crow would; well over twice as far in fact.

Before turning back up the beach to the bike, there's a symbolic act I must carry out. I walk slowly forward to where the last ripples of each breaking wave lap up over the toes of my boots and stand for a moment with the fresh sea breeze buffeting my hair and the salty windblown spray in my nostrils. Reaching deep into my pocket, I pull out the small pebble which the Pacific Ocean had left for me on the beach at Santa Monica, and watch it as it spins briefly through the air before plopping into the Atlantic. I hope you enjoyed the ride, little pebble, you've crossed an entire continent.

I head up the last few miles of the cape to reach the delightful looking little port cum resort of Provincetown, which marks the point from which you need a boat to travel any further. With its harbour filled with colourful fishing boats and its long main street packed with art galleries and restaurants, Provincetown at once strikes me as an artistic and bohemian outpost where it will be most enjoyable and relaxing to spend a few days winding down.

It doesn't take long at all to select a very comfortable, welcoming, and reasonably priced bed and breakfast right on the main street, which I think will make an ideal base for a few days of doing more or less nothing, and definitely not riding a motorbike. So by way of an immediate change of recreational activity, as soon as the bike is suitably tucked away and secured I ditch my bags and head out on foot to Race Point, where I kick off my boots and walk barefoot along the beach for an hour just listening to the swish of the waves, the occasional calling of seagulls, and the wind softly whistling through the grasses on the dunes. I feel like I've arrived at the end of the world, where there's nowhere left to go and nothing more left to see; and in a way, I have. My mind is completely empty, with not a care in the world, and it's a good feeling.

Now if I have a particular favourite when it comes to cuisine, it's seafood. And when it comes to superb seafood, you'd do well to spend a little time anywhere better than Provincetown. The place is surrounded by sea in every direction, and that sea is very well stocked with fish. If it weren't for the slight problem of occasional violent storms, then being a Provincetown fisherman would be a very easy life indeed. This is all the justification I need to splash out on a meal of incomparable excellence at the Lobster Pot restaurant, followed by a good few self-congratulatory beers looking out over the harbour. So here I am. Done it. Feels great.

◆ ◆ ◆

I didn't notice it at all when I first rode down the main street sizing up the various accommodation options on offer, but I now see that virtually every shop, bar, and bed and breakfast in the town, including my own, is sporting a rainbow patterned flag, window sticker, or strange dangly thing with tassels (I believe they are called 'dreamcatchers', though there's no record of a dream ever having been caught). I had absolutely no idea that the Provincetown (or 'P-town' as people often call it) postal district boasts a higher concentration of same-sex households than any other district in the USA. And that's just the permanent residents – in high tourist season, the population rises from 3,000 to as much as 60,000 in what is a 'go to' holiday destination for the LGBTQ community.

It suddenly hits me. This is why George in the bar last night inexplicably turned his back on me at the merest mention of Provincetown! I was heading for P-Town, so in his mind that meant that I must be gay. And if I was gay, then I must be disgustingly promiscuous and certain to make a move on him at any moment. I wonder if he spent the rest of the evening talking with someone else about how sickening it is that you can't even enjoy a drink these days without suffering unwelcome advances from some HIV-ridden pervert?

End of the road.

23rd to 25th May. 0 miles.

Time Out In P-Town.

I t doesn't turn out to be quite the few days of relaxing on the beach which I'd envisaged, as strong winds and horizontal rain lash the town relentlessly by day and whistle and clatter against the windows all night. This is the downside of setting goals or building expectations, and I have to laugh at myself a little. For a long time now I've been forming pictures in my mind of this glorious few days of rest and relaxation, the well-earned reward for completing this journey of mine. Barefoot morning walks along deserted beaches warmed by the spring sunshine, gentle breezes caressing my skin, and the rhythmic swish of small wavelets lapping ashore from a calm sea which sparkles in the sunlight; then taking in a long lazy lunch outside a bar somewhere along the harbour side, chatting with the locals to learn more about the place, perhaps reading a little, and whiling away the afternoons just watching the world go by as I reflect on all the adventures which brought me here. How very pleasant that would all have been. I had a brief and tantalising taste of this idyll with my walk yesterday afternoon, but it turns out that was all I'm going to get.

Anyway, back to reality. I brave the elements by taking an unpleasantly choppy, freezing cold, and entirely unsuccessful whale watching trip on the first of my three days in Provincetown; but not to worry, because a sighting is fully guaranteed and I can keep re-using my ticket again and again until a whale obliges us with an appearance.

It's clear that quite a few of the local maritime community have switched from fishing to pursuing the potentially more lucrative, albeit seasonal, bounty of the tourist trade, as there are no shortage of wooden shacks around the harbour promoting the joys of their whale watching excursions with enticing images of whale tails so close that you could touch them, as they dive beneath the sun-kissed ripples of a calm sea before breaking the surface again with a plume of spray, all for the exclusive delight of a camera brandishing audience decked out in shorts and sunhats. Clearly those glorious summer days I was picturing do actually happen here sometimes, but just not now.

The reality turns out to be a far cry from the glossy advertising though, as the whole outing is a truly awful experience; cooped up in a damp cabin with twenty grey faced tourists all on the brink of projectile vomiting thanks to the violent pitching of the boat and the pervading smell of exhaust fumes, with the only alternative being to stand outside on deck braced against the biting wind while getting a regular dousing with freezing cold salty water. I decide this is the better option in any case, and manage to find a spot where I can stand with my back to the wind and waves and feel a little warmth from the hot exhaust pipe. This lasts all of ten minutes before the boat changes course and ruins everything! The following two days are so wild that all trips are cancelled, but I still have that damn ticket safely tucked away in my desk drawer and I vow that one day I'll return to see a bloody whale off Cape Cod.

I spend some of the next day looking around the Pilgrims Tower and it's museum which actually proves to be fascinating. This part of the world is where, in 1620, the Pilgrim Fathers made their first landfall; and I'd forgotten that one of their number originally came from the little village of Scrooby in England, which my mates and I frequently pedalled the ten miles or so to visit and spend time fishing and getting up to general mischief as kids.

As the weather remains vile, I spend a good deal of time sitting in bars and restaurants too, reading a book or browsing a map and reflecting more on the last few weeks. The locals I chat to, few as they are, are on the whole a very pleasant and hugely diverse bunch. The occasional couple of gay men doing their best to out-camp each other at excessive volume are, admittedly, somewhat irritating (just the kind who reinforce the prejudices of the likes of George). But the general atmosphere around the town is one of contentment, relaxation, and of anyone and everyone being accepted and welcome – whoever they are, wherever they've come from, and whatever their chosen lifestyle.

This would have been a glorious place to unwind if the weather had been sympathetic to my plans, with miles of pristine and largely deserted seashore to roam along and endless sand dunes to sit amongst and read or just lie back and gaze at the sky. But the seaside is the same the world over – it's really crap when it's windy and raining, and instead of enjoying the beach you have to resort to whiling away the hours wandering around the few indoor options available, which of course are all packed because everyone else is in the same boat. It's either that or just spending all day getting steadily pissed. I'm soon tired of the fairly rubbishy gift shops, and it turns out the art isn't up to much on the whole either, so I'm happy that it's time to move on one last time.

Having been here a few days, my belongings have become spread out across the room rather more than they tend to do with the usual one night stays, and so rounding everything up again takes a little longer. But the process also helps me to filter and rationalise things a little, with quite a few instances of 'why the hell have I been wasting luggage space on that thing for the last six weeks?'

26th May. 136 miles.

Riding The Storm.

I load up the bike and bid my lovely hosts farewell, before heading south through a now familiarly drab and damp Provincetown and back onto the open road. It's been very good to switch off for a few days, but the travel itch has, as expected, not left me and it's definitely a great feeling to be moving once more.

The ride back along the cape remains wet but my spirits are high as I can see brighter skies and even some patches of blue ahead of me across the bay, and my wise investment in a pair of cheap neoprene socks from one of P-towns finest purveyors of seaside tatt does prove highly effective at keeping my feet warm. I stick to the faster main roads this time, rather than meandering along the more scenic route through all the little towns next to the coast again, so it's not long before I'm waving goodbye to Cape Cod and its camera shy whales.

As soon as I'm across the canal and onto the mainland, I peel off the dual carriageway and take the much quieter and winding little road which follows the coastline towards Plymouth. The rain has finally passed, and it's a very beautiful ride through heavily wooded countryside with lots of grand looking houses nestling among the trees, although glimpses of the sea are frustratingly infrequent until the road comes right down to the shoreline beyond the sleepy little seaside town of Manomet, whose only claim to fame seems to be that it holds its 4th July celebrations on the 3rd. I've no idea why and the information board doesn't offer any clues either. Maybe they just like to be different.

Arriving at the seafront in Plymouth, I'm met by a glorious scene with thousands of boats moored in the harbour beyond the tourist bustle and the beautifully kept seafront gardens. The clouds have broken, the sun is shining, and the last patches of damp are rapidly drying from the roads and pavements. I've got plenty of time to take a long and leisurely lunch stop, and this looks like the perfect place to spend it.

I park up the bike at the Pilgrim Memorial State Park, which seems the most appropriate place to stop as 'Pilgrim Tourism' appears to be the main focus of activity around these parts, and head off first in search of lunch and a drink before going to examine the famous Plymouth Rock – supposedly marking the exact point where the Pilgrims aboard the Mayflower first set foot on American soil.

It turns out to be a sizeable, but otherwise unre-markable, boulder with the date 1620 carved into its side and an obvious crack right through the middle. The crack happened back in the 18th century when they tried to move it from the beach to the town square, dropping it in the process and breaking it clean in two, and they've not made a particularly neat job of gluing it back together in my opinion. It's now situated back on the beach and surrounded by a rather grand and elaborate granite structure which is quite reminiscent of a Greek temple, presumably to stop anyone trying to steal it.

Reading a little more about it, I'm intrigued to find that the Pilgrims made no mention at all of any such rock in their written accounts of the time, and in fact the first mention of Plymouth Rock marking their landing point didn't appear anywhere until a whop-ping 121 years after the event.

Over on the other side of the park there's an im-pressive looking full-sized replica of the Mayflower – the ship which brought the Pilgrim Fathers to these shores four hundred years ago, and may or may not have bumped into this rock as its bows slid up onto the beach. I sign up for one of the guided tours, and it's all fairly well done and quite authentic, with the exception of the crewman-cum-guide whose bizarre imitation of an English accent is quite something to witness. Dick van Dyke's famously comedic take on the cockney twang in the Mary Poppins film has some serious competition here. He's so hilariously bad that

I find it impossible to actually follow what he's telling us.

After a very pleasant couple of hours in the Plymouth sunshine, I can't put the moment off any longer - it's time to get back on the bike for the very last leg of the journey and ride the final few miles into the heart of Boston, first to find the hire depot where I shall be bidding my trusty steed farewell, and then to search out the nearest hotel ready for a speedy getaway in the morning.

And looking in the direction I'm heading, it seems that the weather is about to have one final and very dramatic part to play in this adventure.

I make a last check of the map and mount up in sunshine, but as the key turns in the ignition I see the first few tell-tale spots of rain spatter onto the fuel tank in front of me. It's just a few drops though, and the sun is still out. What's daunting is how it looks over Boston – the contrast is staggering, as though it's a sunny day here, and yet just a few miles ahead it's the middle of the night.

Immediately I leave Plymouth behind me, the sky rapidly darkens to shades of charcoal, brooding and threatening; the temperature dips sharply, and in the intense gloom ahead I see the first jagged forks of lightning cracking into the ground. As the increasingly heavy raindrops clatter against my helmet and visor, I pull into a convenient layby and hurriedly wriggle into my waterproofs. In just those few seconds the storm has arrived with its full vengeance and the torrential rain is now hammering onto the road and bouncing back up again. I can't stay here as it could take hours to pass, there's no shelter, and I'm going to be drenched in minutes. And that, right there, was the moment my mistake was made; because I could have stayed put, and I should have stayed put – I would have been wet, I would have been cold, and I would have been miserable; but I would also have been safe.

Taking a deep breath, I rev the engine, my face adopts a steely eyed smile, and I blast straight ahead into the full force of the storm. It's pure exhilaration and pumping adrenalin, not to say plain frightening. Huge raindrops, then hailstones, ping and rattle against my helmet and I actually gasp with the pain as they sting my legs so much. Through thick socks, heavy jeans, and a waterproof oversuit, each hailstone stabs sharply into my flesh like a piercing jab from a needle. If these things get any bigger they're going to start breaking things.

The storm is absolutely biblical, wild, intense and terrifying now. All around me the jagged bolts of lightning flash to earth, and deafening claps of thunder drown out the engine, the hail, everything. Spray from the cars makes it near impossible to see anything ahead or behind me, yet I have to try and match the pace as there's no chance that anyone can see the small outline of a bike and rider with only a single and quite feeble rear light to show that I'm here. A few yards ahead and to the side of me, a car suddenly swerves violently as its tyres start to aquaplane on the surface water and it grinds into the metal barriers which separate the carriageways. Then another crashes over the nearside kerb, and another; and I'm pushing on through it all relying on nothing more than luck to get me out of this apocalyptic scene. I could easily be killed if I keep going, and just as easily if I stop and try to shelter.

I've made a terrible mistake for sure. This is a completely crazy place to be on a bike, about as close to suicidal as you can get. But I don't panic, I mustn't, I have to keep my mind focussed and just ride the damn bike, that's all I can do. Sure, I shouldn't be here, but I am, and there's no point dwelling on the whys and wherefores because it's too late for that. I am where I am, and I need to concentrate, keep going. I've got myself into a bad situation, and now I need to get myself out of it again. There's no escape, other than to ride right through the eye of the storm and out the other side.

Luck stays with me and as I press on through the gathering outskirts of Boston, just as quickly as the storm arrived, the dark clouds suddenly begin to part and the sun once again breaks through.

My heart is still pounding, I'm soaked to the skin, mightily relieved at having survived the ordeal, and very happy when I find the bike depot with relative ease. I decide to stop and grab a few cans of beer before hunting for a suitable motel and setting about trying to dry my jeans and boots and jacket for one last time.

Unloading the bike a short time later, I find to my dismay that one of the newly acquired cans has been pierced by something sharp inside the pannier bag, and for fifteen minutes or so a fine intense spray of beer has been liberally applied to all my luggage; and the shirt which I've kept clean for six long weeks ready to travel home in has borne the brunt of this alcoholic pressure wash.

And so it is that fate conspires to deliver me safely through storm and tempest, and to see me spending my last night in America – ironing.

27th May. 1 mile.

Goodbye My Friend.

I t's a very quick run of just a few short blocks back to the bike rental agency where I meet a most amiable chap by the name of Joe, who seems to be a one man band running his small backstreet garage doing general servicing and repairs as well as the rental franchise on the side.

Joe puts his spanner down on the workbench and wipes his hands vigorously with a rag, which I can't help noticing actually seems to make them dirtier than they were before. He then welcomes me with the words 'good job you chose to drop her off this morning man, you shoulda just seen the weather here yesterday afternoon.' He shows not the slightest interest in completing any paperwork or checking the bike over. In truth, he doesn't need to, as it's still running as sweetly as the day I picked it up, nothing has broken or fallen off, and I haven't crashed or even dropped it. All it really needs is a deep clean, a good service, and a new front tyre. He's just interested to hear about my adventure, and is more than happy to shut up shop and drive me to where I can catch a bus to the airport once I've given him the basic outline over a mug of strong coffee.

I take a lingering last look at the bike and pat the fuel tank, as Joe looks at me with a slightly quizzical expression. To him it's just another bike of course, but to me it's so much more. He drops me at the bus station and I thank him and bid him farewell, buy myself a ticket, and just five minutes later I'm on my way to catch my flight home.

I feel very sad to have parted company with the bike, my constant companion for six weeks, which has enabled me to see and experience so much in a way which few others do. Travelling with company can often be difficult, but it's very easy to form a deep bond when your companion doesn't express an opinion or disagree with anything, and just obediently goes along with whatever whim you decide to follow. And through all those thousands of miles, through sun, rain, snow, hail, wind, thunder and lightning, that engine hasn't missed a single beat. I have to salute you, Harley-Davidson; in a world so filled with short-lived and disposable junk, you stick to the principle of building it solid, simple, and reliable. The result is certainly expensive, and with no frills or gadgets to show for the money, but it does its job like very few other things do. It's certainly true to say that Harleys are the Marmite of the biking world - many regard them as oil-spewing dinosaurs, but neither this one nor my own has ever shed a drop; many will mock their truly appalling handling characteristics and cornering ability, not appreciating that they're designed and built for a land which, for the most part, simply doesn't have corners; and while perhaps a little more technology might improve them, and it would be a great bonus if the brakes were good enough to actually stop them, well they just wouldn't really be Harleys then would they? All things considered and duly weighed up, I absolutely love 'em and I wouldn't change a single thing about them.

Once the plane has climbed through the clouds and set its course out across the Atlantic, and the cabin crew have got the trolley into action, I sit back with a satisfied smile and raise a plastic glass of champagne to an incredible adventure which has finally come to an end; and my thoughts turn to the identical bike which waits patiently in my garage back at home.

Where next?

EPILOGUE.

Everything Changes.

I arrived safely home, attended to the laundry and dealt with the pile of post. I then wheeled my own bike out of the garage, headed out for a little ride, and began to ponder that question – where next?

The answer turned out to be a madcap tour of Europe, travelling through fourteen countries in fourteen days; and the trip after that saw me return to America to make the journey which I'd thought about on the very first day of my Route 66 adventure – from Montana across to Seattle and then down the entire west coast highway to San Diego.

I stayed closer to home the next time, making a complete circumnavigation of the coast of Britain, which turned out to be a surprisingly long way!

Heading for foreign lands again, I rode from home to the Sahara Desert and back, and then took a trip around the coastline of Ireland following the spectacular Wild Atlantic Way; while countless shorter trips, mostly around Britain and Europe, continue to fill in the gaps between the big ones. It's safe to say I still have the bug, and I don't suppose it'll ever leave me.

I kept my beloved Harley-Davidson for seventeen years in all, and it never once let me down. I eventually changed it for a BMW R1200GS, a completely different animal and much better suited to long distance travel. But does it have quite the same character? Does it stir the soul in the same way? Of course it doesn't.

And what of Route 66? Has the old road changed over the years? Would it still be as special if you travelled it today?

The world constantly evolves, and so does Route 66. I made this journey in 2005, and if you take the 'same' journey today, it won't be the same. Some of the places I visited or stayed at will have succumbed to decline and closed down, while others which were closed when I passed will by now have been reborn. Some of the people I encountered along the way will have moved on, and some will doubtless have passed away. But others will inevitably have taken their place.

Don't worry about that, because Route 66 is used to change, and it'll be just as exciting and just as rewarding today as it always has been. It's important to remember that this road isn't a museum, it doesn't have a curator whose job it is to preserve it in a particular moment in time, to dust it regularly and keep it looking tidy. Although, in a way, it has lots of curators – all those wonderful people who live and work along the road, each looking after their own little part of it. I take my hat off to them. Before I set out on my journey, I thought it was just going to be about the road and the extraordinary landscapes which it travels through. It hadn't occurred to me that it would be just as much, if not more, about the people that I encountered along the way; and I certainly hadn't expected to learn so much about myself.

If you've ever had even the briefest thought about travelling this extraordinary road, or any other great journey for that matter, then I hope this book might just provide that little extra nudge that turns the dream into reality. If it does, then enjoy the trip!

And if you've never stepped out of the comfort zone of having company around you, if you've never travelled alone and discovered the special qualities which it brings to the journey, then I hope I might also have tempted you to try that too.

You can cover the 2,500 miles of Route 66 with relative ease in a couple of weeks, with enough time to take in most of the highlights. But if you have more time, then I would certainly urge you to use it. I covered 6,400 miles with all my meanderings and of course the sizeable extra leg which took me right across the continent to the east coast, and I spent nearly six weeks doing it.

By all means plan ahead in detail if that's your style, but just remember you may be stifling spontaneity in the process. Since Route 66, I've undertaken many more great road trips and never once arranged anything more than flights or ferries and the first night's accommodation in advance. Despite this, I've never found myself stuck for lodgings or a decent campsite, and the lack of a strict itinerary has allowed me to discover and explore so many hidden gems which I would otherwise have missed. Perhaps equally important, such a flexible approach to a trip makes it easy to adjust to those occasional but inevitable mishaps like punctures or breakdowns or stomach upsets.

To me, a road trip is very much about stepping away from the shackles of the plans and lists and deadlines that plague our everyday lives. It's about having a broad outline in terms of timescale and destination, but largely leaving the day-to-day detail to unfold by chance, always being open to the unexpected opportunities which will undoubtedly present themselves along the way.

But here's the big question. Is it, in fact, this approach to road trips which has ended up shaping my approach to life in general? Or is it my approach to life which has influenced how I tackle these journeys? Of course, the answer is both. That's just the way I'm wired up, and whether it's a motorbike trip, or my work, or life in general, I can't think of anything worse than having it all mapped out down to the very last detail.

I've talked in the book about the kind of people who live their lives with a dogged determination to achieve a pre-determined set of goals, whatever it takes. And they're generally successful people as a result, by whatever measure of success you, or they, care to use. But that just isn't me. I don't really do clearly defined goals; I do curiosity and opportunism. I don't really know what I'm looking for a lot of the time; but when I find it, when I have that 'Ah, this must be the place' moment, I relish having the flexibility to explore and appreciate and learn about whatever it is that I've found, before resuming the journey once more.

And this is why I say 'by all means plan ahead if that's your style'. Because, if that is your style, if you're a goal setter, if you need a schedule or a set of objectives against which to measure progress, then you'd probably hate travelling with me!

Where are we heading today? Hmm, that way looks good.

Where are we staying tonight? No idea.

When are we stopping for lunch? When we're hungry.

How far are we going? Depends what we find along the way.

You could say I lack focus, and that I'm easily distracted. And you'd be right. Except I don't call it a lack of focus, and I don't see it as a problem. It's not as though I have absolutely no plan at all. My plan is to get to the other side of America in six weeks' time, simple as that. So there's definitely a plan of sorts. It just lacks a fair amount of detail, I'm not cocooned within a comfortable safety net of waypoints and timings, and as a result I have complete freedom to discover the, as yet, unknown and grasp the opportunities which it presents. All that's necessary is to embrace the fear, fire up the engine, and hit the road.

AND FINALLY...

I've used made-up names for just a few of the people mentioned in this book; not to protect their identities, but simply because I can't actually remember what they were. Other than that, everything you've read is just as it happened.

I'd particularly like to thank just a few of the characters who helped to make my journey so special:

Andrea Pruett, who at the time of publication is still welcoming visitors to the Bagdad Café with that bright cheerful smile of hers. Johnie Calahan, who gave up the Uranium Café and now lives with his family and spends lots of time with his grandchildren; it sounds like he's happy. Bill Dunkus, still running Interstate Motorcycles and now an author too; thanks for fixing my puncture. And Chris from the Missouri Hick, my knight in shining armour. The guy in the bar full of bras, he never told me his name and it's been impossible to trace him, but I enjoyed meeting you whoever you are. Fran Houser at the Midpoint, who sold up and moved on but left the café in capable hands. Ron at the Wellington Willows, who's also moved on, and also left the business in good hands. And last but not least, to that wonderful Harley-Davidson Dyna Wide Glide, registration 17L7294, without which none of it could have happened.

Can I ask a huge favour? If you've enjoyed the book, please will you take a moment to leave me a review? Reviews help so much in spreading the word to a wider audience, as well as making those endless hours slaving over a keyboard seem even more worthwhile, and they are massively appreciated.

If you'd like to see more pictures of this and other road trips, or to contact me about anything, then you can do so at www.richardsharp.co.uk

Thank you, and safe travels.

ABOUT THE AUTHOR

Richard Sharp

I was just an ordinary sales rep leading an ordinary life when, with half an hour to kill before a meeting, I walked into a motorcycle dealership in London to have a mooch around and see if there was a free coffee on offer.

What happened next would change my life forever.

Then and there, I determined to buy the glistening machine I saw displayed in the centre of the showroom. The only problem was that I'd never ridden a motorcycle before.

So at the age of forty I set about learning to ride and passing my test, duly became the proud owner of that fabulous Harley-Davidson Dyna Wide Glide motorcycle, and soon discovered the irresistible lure of the 'road trip'.

Fifteen years later, and with motorcycle adventures through more than 25 countries spanning 4 continents under my belt, I've now dug out my travel diaries and begun to share these fantastic journeys with this tale of my epic adventure across America, made just two years after sitting astride a bike for the very first time.

I live in the English Lake District and divide my time between earning a living, writing, and, of course, motorcycling. I kept the Harley for 17 years and shed quite a few tears when I finally let it go. I now ride a BMW R1200GS (aka, 'Ewan & Charlie bike'); a far more capable allrounder with much more tech, and certainly a more appropriate bike for big adventures - but it'll never stir my soul quite like the Harley did.

Printed in Great Britain
by Amazon